Fragile Resurrection

Fragile Resurrection

Practicing Hope after Domestic Violence

Ashley E. Theuring

FOREWORD BY
Nancy Pineda-Madrid

CASCADE *Books* · Eugene, Oregon

FRAGILE RESURRECTION
Practicing Hope after Domestic Violence

Cascade Books
An Imprint of Wipf and Stock Publishers
199 W. 8th Ave., Suite 3
Eugene, OR 97401

www.wipfandstock.com

PAPERBACK ISBN: 978-1-7252-6014-6
HARDCOVER ISBN: 978-1-7252-6009-2
EBOOK ISBN: 978-1-7252-6012-2

Cataloguing-in-Publication data:

Names: Theuring, Ashley E., author. | Pineda-Madrid, Nancy, foreword.

Title: Fragile resurrection : practicing hope after domestic violence / Ashley E. Theuring ; foreword by Nancy Pineda-Madrid.

Description: Eugene, OR: Cascade Books, 2021. | Includes bibliographical references and index.

Identifiers: ISBN: 978-1-7252-6014-6 (PAPERBACK). | ISBN: 978-1-7252-6009-2 (HARDCOVER). | ISBN: 978-1-7252-6012-2 (EBOOK).

Subjects: LCSH: Domestic violence. | Theology of Hope. | Resurrection.

Classification: BV4445.5 T55 2021 (print). | BV4445.5 (ebook).

To Chris,
without whom I would have certainly lost my mind . . .

Contents

Foreword

NANCY PINEDA-MADRID

MARTIN LUTHER ONCE FAMOUSLY remarked, "All theology begins with suffering." To be sure, extreme suffering poses the greatest threat to belief in a good and loving God, particularly the suffering of the innocent. And, while much theological ink has been spent in attempts to offer a credible response to why God allows destructive and protracted suffering to continue, nonetheless, every theological response, to a greater or lesser degree, fails. In the end, theology is reduced to silence. Even so, the enduring question of suffering remains, and in every era, theologians continue their endeavor to shed more light on this elusive enigma.

For almost two millennia, theologians have considered human suffering with great empathy and insightfulness, but quite rarely with attention to the difference gender makes. Theologians have addressed the suffering of men and the suffering of women as a very serious, singular reality, which tacitly normalizes men's experience of suffering and erroneously presumes the inclusion of women's experience. As Ivone Gebara has pointedly noted, men's suffering is generally understood to be in service of some greater cause (like the nation-state, the church, the field of medicine, racial justice in society, and the like). As such, men's suffering entails heroic sacrifice on behalf of others, and therefore, is to be revered in the *public sphere*. In contrast, women's suffering is generally understood through the lens of an "ideology of sacrifice, imposed by patriarchal culture" and in the *private sphere* of home life. Women are encouraged to follow Jesus by taking up their crosses in a manner that silences and victimizes women, encouraging "them in domestic and familial martyrdom."[1] Women's suffering is perceived to be more a private duty than a public heroic undertaking. So while suffering can and does destroy the lives of women and men, women far more often find themselves in situations of greater vulnerability, invisibility, and isolation, making their experience of suffering more acutely destructive of their subjectivity and sense of self.

Domestic violence plagues women almost exclusively, making the suffering it causes an experience known by women and their children. This suffering is among the most isolating and invisible precisely because it occurs in the privacy of the home, characteristics that increase exponentially in the lives of immigrant women who lack documentation and so find themselves forced to remain in hiding or increase their risk of deportation. A theologian with prescient insights, Ashley Theuring recognizes not only the isolation so characteristic of survivors of domestic violence but she is also one who knows the ways that COVID-19, the 2020 economic downturn, and sharply increasing unemployment coalesce to exacerbate phenomena of domestic violence, social isolation, and hopelessness for survivors. Indeed, immigrant women survivors of domestic violence know acute suffering and horrific trauma. To be sure, male perpetrators may also suffer, however, they are in every respect quite substantially less vulnerable to the consequences of the trauma they cause.

Theuring rightly identifies immigrant women survivors of domestic violence, a "crucified people," meaning they are more than a random collection of women who know suffering. Rather, they are particular group of women, who because of their "shared historical reality" owe their crucifixion to society's structures and systems designed to benefit the powerful, the underside of which leads to the crucifixion of the poor. As Ignacio Ellacuría once eloquently wrote: "This crucified people represents the historical continuation of the servant of Yahweh, who is forever being stripped of his human features by the sin of the world, who is forever being despoiled of everything by the powerful of this world, who is forever being robbed of life, especially of life."[2] In reading Theuring's theology, one comes to understand something of Jesus' crucifixion and resurrection. Furthermore, the meaning of Jesus' crucifixion becomes distorted,

---

1. Gebara, *Out of the Depths*, 88–89, 107.

2. Ellacuría, "Discernir 'El Signo' de los Tiempos," 133–35. The English translation is from Burke, "The Crucified People," 124.

caricatured, and diminished when it is not linked to the crucified people of our time as well as of every age. We may wonder, what does it mean to believe in a God of hope and of resurrection when the "crucified people" of our time are the victims of domestic violence? When this crucified people are women—brown, poor, without documentation? Theuring dares to consider nothing less. For well over a decade, in my theology, I have wrestled with this same question as I have confronted the assassinations of women victims of feminicide.[3] To identify groups of women as "a crucified people" confronts the Christian tradition in a fundamental way, requiring a radical rethinking of Christological questions and themes—crucifixion, resurrection, and hope—as Theuring has begun to do in these pages.

To place poor, brown, immigrant women, survivors of domestic violence at the very center of theologizing as Theuring has done here, transforms theological thinking and transforms ministerial practice. Such reflects that for Theuring, an ethical commitment is integral to her theological claims. It links the material condition of women's bodies to the condition of the whole social body of the human community. This line of thinking means that to abuse and destroy poor, brown, immigrant women's bodies is to defame the incarnation of Jesus Christ. And, if we believe that through Jesus Christ's incarnation all of humanity knows its unity (its oneness) then whatever we do that violates or oppresses human beings—survivors of domestic violence—this threatens our communion with one another as it defames the body of Christ. Yet, Theuring takes this a step further.

Not only does Theuring break new theological ground, her work likewise transforms ministerial practice. At the center of this work is Theuring's accompaniment of the immigrant women of House of Peace, located in the greater Chicago area. The residents and their children have survived domestic violence, but Theuring asks, what would the journey toward healing look like? What would it mean to practice fragile resurrection? She spent time accompanying a group of immigrant women as they painted their stories, tracing their experience of crucifixion, their tentative steps toward hope, steps made possible through practices of resurrection. This work is one ever mindful of the chasm between the world as it is and the world as it should be, knowing always that healing is a difficult and fraught journey, on the best days, one that discovers a

---

3. Pineda-Madrid, *Suffering and Salvation in Ciudad Juárez*.

fragile hope. Theuring, like the women of the gospels, invites us to the ambiguous space of the empty tomb where these women live; through their guidance we may just catch a glimpse of the fragile resurrection.

Nancy Pineda-Madrid
T. Marie Chilton Chair of Catholic Theology
Loyola Marymount University
November 25, 2020
International Day for the Elimination of Violence against Women

Introduction

WE LIVE IN AN era of increasing accountability. However, books, news stories, the #metoo movement, and other signs of rising public awareness around issues of abuse have not stopped the reality that is domestic violence. Domestic violence continues in the privacy of our homes and personal relationships. In 2020, the required isolation and disconnection caused by COVID-19, has shed a light on the reality hiding in our communities. With the rising stress of a global pandemic, social distancing, job-loss, and restrictions on community resources, domestic violence and abuse in the home has surged globally.[1] Domestic violence disrupts survivors' sense of agency, connection to others, and imagined futures, through the imbalance of power and control within an intimate relationship. Since domestic violence is a significant life experience for one-third of all women around the world, it becomes a logical center for theological reflection and discussion. While feminist theologians have continued to place the experience of domestic violence as an important dialogue partner for theology, the conversation cannot remain solely centered around diagnosing and framing domestic violence as a theological problem. In this book, I move this conversation forward through the exploration of healing practices after domestic violence and their implications for our theologies of hope.

This book began to first take shape in the fall of 2013. I was finishing my doctoral course work in Boston and looking for fieldwork sites and communities of healing to ground and inform my theological research. A close friend and colleague of mine from back home in Cincinnati called while I was commuting home from class one day. She spoke excitedly about a domestic violence community she had traveled to Chicago to visit. "You have to go. This place is different." She had told me. She knew

1. Taub, "A New Covid-19 Crisis."

my background as a domestic violence advocate, and more importantly she knew my frustrations with the operation of many domestic violence shelters, which often lack imagination around practices of creating community.

One month later, I was on a plane to House of Peace. I would return to Waukegan, a northern suburb of Chicago, several times over the next three years for a couple days or a week at a time. During my first few visits during the fall 2013 and spring 2014, I interviewed former residents, volunteers, the director Aida, and her assistant director Vanessa. At the time my research questions mostly focused on spirituality, religious practices, domestic violence, and healing. Aida offered a wealth of knowledge about the community and the prospect of working together on these questions excited her. She was (and remains) an integral part of this project, setting up interviews for me, patiently answering my many questions, providing me with a spare room in the house to stay, and all around making me feel welcome.

During my first visit to House of Peace, Aida had given me an oral history of the shelter and the larger social services project that oversaw the shelter, Community Social Services. At the time, the Catholic Church diocese of Waukegan supervised the project. Aida explained that the Most Blessed Trinity parish is predominantly made up of immigrants, estimating about 85 percent of parishioners were specifically Mexican immigrants. The Catholic diocese combined three separate church communities to create the parish, in the hopes of pooling resources and being able to provide better services to this extremely impoverished area of Chicago. At the time of our initial interviews, this parish had an unknown number of parishioners with over 7,000 people attending mass on any given Sunday.

The large size of the parish acts as both a strength and an obstacle for the community. The church can pull on the seemingly endless skills and gifts of the community, and yet the high rates of poverty result in a dearth of financial resources. The community started the domestic violence project in 2011 in order to address the absence of domestic violence services for both survivors and perpetrators. Before the community took on this issue, these men and women were severely under-served because of language barriers and the neighborhood's lack of social service funding in general. Many of the women who stay at House of Peace, are unable to stay at other shelters because of their lack of documentation. As both immigrants and survivors of abuse, these women face marginalization that is intersectional to their race, gender, and class, living much of their daily lives under the threats of deportation, homelessness, and an abusive partner.

Almost immediately, I could see what my colleague had meant about the uniqueness of House of Peace. The focus on intentional communal living at the center of House of Peace's mission gives this place little resemblance to other domestic violence shelters. At the insistence of Aida, the program is a selective six-month residency, with a maximum of six families staying at the house at one time. At the time the pastor had asked Aida to direct the shelter, her first response had been hesitation. "I had worked in shelters before and . . . I don't have a lot of faith about the transformation that happens," she explained to me. She continued, "But the pastor asked me to really try and to think about a model—a kind of a way in which a shelter might be able to work, might actually be a place where true transformation could be facilitated." Aida had seen this as a "challenging invitation" and ultimately decided to direct House of Peace. She believed that creating a family-like community was going to be a central aspect to a successful shelter.

Upon entering the actual building, House of Peace certainly feels more like a family home than "a shelter." My first visit to the house naturally included a tour of the old-rectory-turned-shelter. We began in the large spotless kitchen, which included industrial appliances accommodating the large number of people in the house, while also encouraging shared meals, with a single kitchen table. We wound through the house. There were communal spaces, some office space for Aida and Vanessa, bedrooms that were large enough for the mothers with their children, and several communal bathrooms. Over 200 volunteers, including local Boy Scout troops and high school tennis teams, helped to renovate, paint, decorate, and furnish the house, giving it a homey, eclectic aesthetic.

The tour ended in the dining room, the physical center of the house and the heart of life at House Peace. Later that evening the residents of the house would all gather around the long wooden table and share in a communal meal, a delicious red pozole, which had been cooking in a capacious stockpot on the stove all day. The half-dozen or so children would run in and out of the dining-room laughing and shouting, checking to see if their bowl of stew had cooled enough to take a few gulps before running back into the living room with their new housemates. But that would all happen later; at the moment, the house sat mostly empty with only a few women and their children coming or going at a time.

The survivors spend much of their time focused on both the practical aspects of recovering from domestic violence—securing documentation, finding a new place to live, attending court—as well as the emotional aspects of healing. This healing journey takes many forms and there are a number of practices that become central to the flow of life in the house. The women cook together, eat together, care for each other and each other's children, create and maintain a living space together, dance together (weekly Zumba), and attend a weekly support group together. Many of these seemingly mundane tasks become practices of healing, helping to establish safety, routine, and support for the community at the house. By the following year, in fall of 2014, I began to focus my research around the question of hope after domestic violence.

House of Peace as "the Crucified Ones" of Today

The experiences and testimonies of the survivor-residents at House of Peace are integral to the theological text you hold in your hand. Their stories are not only significant because of their experiences as survivors of domestic violence, but also their status as poor, immigrant women. Liberation theologians argue that the poor and oppressed share a deep connection with Jesus' life, suffering, and death as victims of structural oppression. This connection makes the lives and voices of the marginalized important sources of theological insights and key to understanding salvation. The survivors at House of Peace experience systemic oppression in multiple and interconnected ways based on their nationality, class, and gender. The triple marginalization of these women results in racialized deportation, housing insecurity, and domestic violence. The women at House of Peace are compelling conversation partners for a theological investigation into hope after trauma, because of their unique experiences as extremely marginalized in our society and their insights into structural oppression.

My choice to engage the experiences and voices of the women at House of Peace in my investigation of hope after trauma stems from my theological commitment to the "preferential option for the poor." This Catholic social teaching focuses us towards privileging both the practical needs of the poor and their theological insights as a community, who share their experiences of oppression and marginalization with those whom Jesus served during his life. Liberation theologian, Jesuit, and martyr, Ignacio Ellacuría, names the poor and oppressed the "crucified ones" of today. In his essay, "The Crucified People," Ellacuría connects the tradition of the suffering servant found throughout the Hebrew Bible, and featured prominently in Second Isaiah, to both the person of Jesus and the oppressed of today. While the term "crucified ones" is amorphous, Ellacuría does give us a few key aspects of how to define this term today; specifically, the crucified people of today are from the "third world," "an oppressed class," and are "struggling for justice." Most significantly, Ellacuría argues that the poor of today, "the crucified ones," are "a principle of salvation for the entire world."[2] Fellow Jesuit and friend, Jon Sobrino, explains the connection of the poor to the salvation of the world. He writes that "The light that comes from the poor is what makes it possible to overcome voluntary blindness. This light can awaken people from the dogmatic dream to which the West has succumbed: the dream about its own reality."[3] The "crucified ones" of today, those who are poor, marginalized, and oppressed, show us where our systems and structures as a society have failed or in some cases perpetrated evil. We are often too entrenched in these systems to see their evils and sins, but the poor and oppressed have fallen outside these systems in ways that reveal their flaws. In order to embody flourishing and fully realize the Kin-dom of God in our lived experience, we must re-imagine our society in light of what the poor experience.

For us to incorporate the voices and experiences of the poor into our theological works, theologians turn to qualitative methods. Through interviews and other ethnographic methods of observations and investigation, researchers can bring the voices of the "crucified ones," as an authoritative theological source, into their discernment. Rather than just representatives of a minority community, the marginalized become significant co-authors in theological construction.[4] The crucified ones of today, as the central subjects of theological investigation, must be part of the knowledge production, or we risk reinforcing the status quo. As

2. Ellacuría, "The Crucified People."

3. Sobrino, *No Salvation*, 60–61.

4. This is not a unique claim. For example, rather than focusing on constructing theology *for* communities of poor women that concerned her, or following a qualitative method that turns the experiences of her community into statistics, Ada María Isasi-Díaz focuses on individual voices and gives space for Hispanic women collaborators to exercise their agency and shape the understanding of their own theological claims and practices. Isasi-Díaz, *En la Lucha*, 176.

Sobrino highlighted above, the poor and marginalized are important story-tellers, because their experiences are dangerous memories that reveal that the "normal," middle-class life is an illusion of stability. From femicide in Ciudad Juarez to genocide in Armenia, the non-narrative, often "illogical," and disturbing nature of trauma experienced by humanity around the world has often subverted our trust in the systems and structures that maintain inequality globally.[5] Because these narratives question the status quo, they are dangerous to those in power, who often attempt to silence them.

When we think about the "crucified ones" of today, the domestic violence survivors of House of Peace fit many of these criteria. Their experiences as survivors of violence in addition to their status as immigrant women make them crucial co-authors to the theological investigations at the heart of this book. Their survival and flourishing subvert the narratives of death and marginalization in our current society. When we consider the question of hope after trauma, the unending nature of trauma becomes a problem. The question becomes: "*How* do we hope when our suffering has left us permanently changed?" Our understanding of hope must be flexible enough to stretch over the traumatic event and the new life we make on the other side. If we turn to the particular context of domestic violence, another problem theologians face when constructing hope is the isolating nature of abuse. Abusers often use tactics that isolate survivors from their networks of support, friends, and families, as well as destroy a survivors ability to trust themselves. Theologies of salvation often turn to internal sources of hope, found in the self, or external sources of hope, found in others.[6] If we mediate hope through the self and others, how do survivors of domestic violence experience hope?

In my search for the answers to these questions, I conducted interviews with five former residents of House of Peace.[7] Our conversations

---

5. Pineda-Madrid, *Suffering and Salvation*; and Keshgegian, *Redeeming Memories*.

6. For example, theologian Jennifer Beste pushes against Karl Rahner's theology of freedom in light of the experiences of incest survivors. Drawing on her work with survivors, Beste finds that grace is socially mediated, and that the experiences of survivors inhibit their ability to choose grace (as Rahner argues). For this reason, it is only through supportive relationships with others that we can access our true relationship with the Divine. See Beste, *God and the Victim*.

7. The interviews were each an hour in length and were structured with some openended, follow-up questions. Each interview was recorded, and conducted through an interpreter, in a private meeting space at House of Peace. The director of the house initially approached each interviewee to gauge interest in being interviewed

focused on the women's memories of their stay at House of Peace, the daily practices and relationships that characterized their time in the house. All five women were survivors of domestic violence, native Spanish speakers, and parishioners of the local Catholic church. During the interviews, I worked closely with an interpreter, Nohemi, who volunteered in the house and knew many of the residents. She also translated and transcribed the interview transcripts and was a close research partner throughout the process of interpreting the data.

Along with the interviews, the director, Aida, gave me access to ten narratives, known as "Resurrection Stories" written by House of Peace residents near the end of their stays. The women designed and painted wooden crosses to represent their own healing journeys. They then wrote a narrative, which was displayed next to their cross. As part of an ongoing public exhibit curated by House of Peace, these crosses and narratives have been on display at a number of events since their creation. I first saw and read the "Resurrection Stories" during a community event, where House of Peace had a table set up at a community center in Waukegan. This event took place during one of my stays at the house and I enlisted to help transport and set up the exhibit of the "Resurrection Stories" and their corresponding crosses.

The "Resurrection Stories" project gives survivors an opportunity to re-narrate and re-imagine their journey of suffering and healing, within the framework of the cross and resurrection narratives. For many of the women I interviewed, this practice was a powerful part of their healing process and provided them the opportunity and space to make art. Several of the survivors indicated that painting, especially the "Resurrection Stories'" crosses, was one of their favorite activities during their stay. One survivor I spoke with, Martina, smiled as she reflected on her experiences of painting and creating art during her stay at the shelter. Martina had never painted before, and certainly had never thought of painting as a healing practice. But the presence of a kind and patient teacher, "a beautiful person, with a huge heart," in combination with the space and

---

about their experience at the house. The director chose interviewees who were already graduates of the program, had availability during my stay, and a willingness to speak on the subject. The director explained the interview was part of a theological research project looking at healing after trauma and their testimonies might be used in published works.

opportunity to paint, helped to cultivate a new creative practice—a practice that Martina described as "painting her soul."[8]

This opportunity to spend time making art is not only a unique one that many of the women appreciate, but it also introduces them to a practice that is transformative in its ability to calm their minds. Martina described her time painting as a moment in which she could just forget about her problems, "forget about all those bad things." Painting not only helped Martina to narrate her healing journey, but it also brought her to a mental space where she had the opportunity to momentarily "forget" about her experiences of suffering. Another survivor I spoke with, Abril, also found painting to have a calming effect on her. She describes the specific "Resurrection Stories" project as the most important project they worked on while at the house, noting that it helped to clear her mind. She explained to me her sense of peace when working on this project, describing her concentration and her ability to be in the present moment of painting and writing. The meditative, calming space that the "Resurrection Stories" create for the residents at House of Peace, provides both space to re-narrate and heal their trauma. The painting and writing become silent and embodied practices, creating a space to hold the survivor in their healing journey.

My findings and theological claims throughout this book are not intended to depict broad sociological findings about survivors of trauma. The sample-size and specificity of my qualitative research with House of Peace can not support universal claims about religious coping, domestic violence, or trauma. Rather, my intention in turning to the few and particular voices of the women at House of Peace is to maintain the integrity of each individual's insights and authoritative voice. These women are theologians in their own right, utilizing theological language to name their experiences. In the same way that I would engage the work of another theologian, I do not turn to their testimonies uncritically, but rather listen to their insights in dialogue with the Christian tradition and our larger context.

A Sacramental Methodology

Theologians have historically turned to our lived experiences as one of the classical sources of truth. Even moments of trauma can be mediators

8. Martina, interviewed by Ashley Theuring.

for Divine presence or reveal the deeper nature of creation. For this book, we will look to the example of domestic violence recovery in the experience of the women of House of Peace. And by turning to the experiences of the survivors at House of Peace, I hope to ground my theological investigation in the context of the "crucified peoples." Rather than a miraculous, inbreaking of the Divine that brings healing and recovery, we will find that God's presence and the practice of hope after trauma is revealed in the mundane and intimate parts of daily life for these women. Hope is radically accessible not because of its overwhelming power, but because of its fragility. Throughout this book, I construct fragile hope as a practice that reflects the everyday, informed by the lives and testimonies of domestic violence survivors. Theological constructions not grounded in the everyday risk creating incomplete or even false theologies. But how do theologians access this crucial theological source?

Theologians can collect and integrate the data of lived experience into their theological investigations using practical theology, ethnography, and qualitative research methods. Interviews, observations, testimonies, and other forms of story-telling turn our daily lives into living texts. Theologians can then work with these texts in similar ways they would work with scripture or theological writings. The sacramental nature of creation and our lives reveals the Divine just below the surface, and when we ignore this important source of theological insight, theologians risk sketching an incomplete or false picture of the world. The importance of our daily lives is particularly significant for those living and working within traditions that hold a sacramental understanding of human experience.[9] Within Catholic theology, since the Second Vatican Council, our daily lives have resurfaced as an important theological source.

The everyday faith and practices of the community, known as *sensus fidelium*, or the sense of the faithful, returned to the Catholic imagination after the Vatican II document, *Lumen gentium*. This document describes the church as the "people of God" and the role of the laity, in addition to clergy, as part of the church community. *Lumen gentium* uses the term "common priesthood" to highlight the theological authority accessible in the lived experience of all humanity. God endows the laity with revelatory authority through grace. *Sensus fidelium* is not the same as majority

9. The volume *Invitation to Practical Theology: Catholic Voices and Visions* edited by Claire Wolfteich, moves to uncover the practical theological aspects of the Catholic tradition as well as make a particularly Catholic contribution to the field of practical theology. See Wolfteich, *Invitation to Practical Theology*.

rule or public opinion. The Catholic Church's 2014 report on the sense of the faithful warned against the uncritical acceptance of "common sense." This report called theologians to listen and critically engage the lived experience of laity and discern where "cultural factors have left their mark."[10] "Cultural factors," such as capitalism or patriarchy, shape humanity and our sense of truth, God, morality, etc. Our lived experience is not without context, and societal structures of evil affect us in ways that are deep and difficult for us to discern.

As theologians engage the voices of the "people of God," they can use ethnographic and qualitative methods to help bring these voices into conversation with scripture, the magisterium, and traditional systematic writings. These methods allow us to access and listen to the revelatory authority our lives hold. But we cannot engage these methods uncritically. The sense of the faithful is not the same as popular public opinion. And majority opinion is not the same as revelation. But which source, the practices of the laity or the tradition of the Church, has more authority? This is a false dichotomy, which empirical methods can sometimes create. The question is not "which is right?," practice or tradition, but rather "how must they both change?" Empirical methods often make the mistake of treating one of these sides as normative. For example, an inductive method focuses on "what *is*," treating the contextual practice as the norm that should shape our tradition and beliefs. This method ignores the effects of structural and cultural evils, such as patriarchy, on our own practices.[11] On the other side of the argument, there is a deductive method that holds tradition up as normative and asks "what *should* be." This methodology treats tradition as fixed, unchanging, and complete, ignoring the role of the Holy Spirit and revelation. Both methodologies are problematic.

In this book, I follow an abductive methodology, often used in pastoral care and religious education, but applied to practical theology by Annemie Dillen and Robert Mager.[12] Rather than asking "what *is*" or "what *should* be," an abductive approach looks at "what *could* be," ultimately utilizing a methodology of imagination. Dillen and Mager write that an abductive approach is able to "interact both with new knowledge from practice/experience and with alternative interpretations, so that

---

10. International Theological Commission. "Sensus Fidei." Paragraph 114.

11. Ormerod, "*Sensus Fidei* and Sociology," 100.

12. Peirce, "How to Make our Ideas Clear"; Hermans, "Abductive Hermeneutics."

what was previously present but hidden in the practices/experiences comes to light, revealing in fact new dimensions."[13] Both practice and tradition are invited into a relationship of change and mutual discernment. In this book, I do not treat practice or tradition as normative, but rather bring them into a dialogue of "conversion."[14] A sacramental worldview, which is open to the presence of God, grace, and revelation, embraces the idea that both tradition and practices have been affected by structural evils, like patriarchy, and must be healed. Through the practical theological method I use in this book, "both practices and theories/traditions are critically challenged to evolve."[15]

In order to critically engage both practices and tradition in a way that challenges both to grow beyond their cultural contexts, I return to the ethical principle of the "crucified people." As we discussed above, the lives of the poor and their experiences of oppression, as the "crucified people" of today, reveal the structural and cultural evils that have taken root in our society, as well as our churches. When we construct theology from the vantage point of those in power, our theology reinforces the status quo. But as theologians and the larger community bring the bodies, voices, and experiences of the poor and oppressed to the center of the conversation, subverting those with earthly power, we can re-imagine both our practices and tradition in light of what they reveal.

Historically, the Church has failed in its response to domestic violence, making the voices and experiences of the women at House of Peace even more significant in their contributions to theology. Survivors of domestic violence are not only affected by the structural evils within our society, but also the toxic theological responses that have unfortunately dominated Church response, including discouraging women from leaving their abusive husbands. Only recently has training for clergy and pastoral leaders on domestic violence been implemented more systematically.[16] While domestic violence has been named a theological problem,

---

13. Dillen and Mager, "Research in Practical Theology," 323.

14. Dillen and Mager, "Research in Practical Theology," 323.

15. Dillen and Mager, "Research in Practical Theology," 324.

16. Studies show that while many survivors of domestic violence turn to religious communities and pastoral leaders, most survivors who reach out to religious authorities leave dissatisfied with the experience, citing issues such as, being given bad advice (i.e. wear him out with sex), that the clergy member had little to no idea how to respond, or even being accused by the clergy member of lying. See Nason-Clark, *The Battered Wife*, 41. and Horton and Williamson, *Abuse and Religion*.

theologians must continue to look at how this experience may challenge specific theological ideas such as hope.

Chapter Summaries

This book begins with a survey of political and liberation theologies of hope as resources for responding to domestic violence and consequential trauma. Chapter 1 engages several of the most influential theologians who have shaped the historical conversation on theological hope, thinkers such as Johann Metz, Jürgen Moltmann, Jon Sobrino, Ada Maria Isasi-Díaz, Roger Haight, Elizabeth Johnson, Shawn Copeland, and Elaine Crawford. Together these theologians construct hope as holistic, including the individual and the community in this work of embodying God's promise for freedom and flourishing of all. The goal of this chapter is to trace the conversation and themes that make up theological hope and begin to highlight hope's contextual nature. The major constructive contribution of this book builds on the theological foundation set forth in this chapter.

Chapter 2 continues with an overview of the problem of domestic violence and theology's engagement with gender-based abuse, summarizing the conversation around domestic violence in the field of theology. After a statistical and systemic overview of the issue of domestic violence itself, this chapter gives a summary of early feminist scholarship, engaging theologians such as Rosemary Radford Reuther and Marie Fortune, who worked to diagnose domestic violence as a theological issue. Next, this chapter gives an ecumenical outline of the church's historical engagement with domestic violence, exploring both church documents and public stances on relationships, marriage, and family, highlighting the church's lack of direct response and engagement with this issue. This chapter also describes the influences of trauma theologians to the theological conversation around domestic violence. The purpose of this chapter is to argue the importance of moving the church and theologians' responses to domestic violence forward, beyond clergy and pastoral education and towards active community engagement.

Chapter 3 turns to the Gospel of Mark's Empty Tomb resurrection account, which is uniquely suited to engage questions of trauma and abuse, because the Markan community's experience of trauma shaped its female-focused and "unending" narrative. This chapter ultimately brings forth a trauma informed account of the resurrection, engaging Latina theologians, Ivone Gebara and Nancy Pineda-Madrid, who present hope as what emerges through embodied practices of resistance. Their vision of fragile redemption and their contextualization of the cross and resurrection yield insights for a constructive feminist reading of resurrection, facilitating the constructive work in the following chapters.

Chapter 4 re-imagines the Empty Tomb narrative and narratives of resurrection through the lens of domestic violence and healing after trauma, engaging the voices of the House of Peace survivors of domestic violence. This chapter reveals the nature of hope and resurrection after domestic violence as "embodied imaginative hope." This hope is more fully developed in the final chapter.

Chapter 5 defines hope after domestic violence as a practice that 1) names evil and suffering while exploring possible action for the here and now, 2) uses imagination to open the future while leaving room for the possible return of trauma, and 3) most significantly, healthy relationships and the mundane tasks of life mediate it. The conclusion further develops this book's contributions to academic theology and the wider church, highlighting future implications for the concept of "embodied imaginative hope" within churches and communities responding to trauma.

Acknowledgments

There are several people and organizations to which I and this book are greatly indebted. First and foremost, I would like to thank the women of House of Peace of Chicago, who were willing to share their stories of suffering and healing with me. Without their insights into hope and healing after trauma this project would not have been possible. The director of House of Peace, Aida Segura, was also an instrumental supporter of this project and someone to whom I am deeply indebted for her boundless hospitality. Also, I would like to thank Nohemi Melgarejo, who was a patient and diligent interpreter, collaborator, and friend throughout this project as well.

This book began as a dissertation and was heavily influenced and supported by my advisor and readers for this project, Shelly Rambo (advisor), Pamela Lightsey (first reader), and Nancy Pineda-Madrid (second reader). These three scholars provided support and feedback that was integral to the shaping and reshaping of this project over several years. I would also like to thank my colleagues at Boston University who got me through my doctoral work, especially Tim Synder and Kate Common for their honest feedback, encouragement, and friendly competition.

The work of transforming a dissertation into something people might want to read is grueling. After the initial dissertation phase, this project was heavily supported by my colleagues and mentors at Xavier University, who have believed in and encouraged me over the past ten years. A special thanks to those who gave me feedback on this particular project: Gillian Ahlgren, Art Dewey, Marcus Mescher, Anna Miller, and Kristine Suna-Koro.

I would also like to thank my loving and supportive husband, Chris Cerone, as well as our families (especially both of our moms), for all their encouragement and support over the years. And finally, with a heavy heart, I want to especially thank my late maternal grandfather, Glenn "Poppy" Weist, who financially supported many years of my education and made much of this possible. He was more excited about this book being published than anyone.

I

Tracing Theological Hope

"Hope functions as a bridge between oppression and liberation."
—A. ELAINE BROWN CRAWFORD[1]

IN ORDER TO ANSWER the question, "what constitutes hope after domestic violence?" I will begin with a survey of modern hope theologies that have shaped the Christian church and the academy in the United States. Below, I engage several of the most influential theologians who have participated in the historical conversation on theological hope, thinkers such as Johann Metz, Jürgen Moltmann, Jon Sobrino, Ada Maria Isasi-Díaz, Roger Haight, Elizabeth Johnson, Shawn Copeland, and Elaine Crawford. Together these theologians construct hope as holistic, including the individual and the community in this work of embodying God's promise for freedom and flourishing of all. My goal in this chapter is to trace the conversation and themes that make up theological hope and highlight hope's contextual nature.

Hope is contextually determined. The historical setting, the type of suffering, and the community all shape how hope is understood, experienced, and embodied. The theological expressions of hope in German political theologies, Latin American liberationist theologies, American Catholic theologies, and womanist theologies, for example, differ greatly because of their varying contexts and experiences of suffering. At the same time, the larger Christian tradition, practices, and stories provide

1. Crawford, *Hope in the Holler*, 112.

roots and grounding for many of the shared themes and connections within these differing conversations. In the case of Christian hope, the central influences of Jesus' crucifixion and resurrection bridges these contextually different expressions of hope.

Scholars often cite the modern academic theological conversation around hope to have begun with the wave of political theologies that developed in Germany immediately after the fall of the Third Reich. The problem with this account is that it ignores the larger global conversation that took place at the turn of the modern era. Kwok Pui Lan critiques this narration, pointing to the political theological works of advocates and theologians like Wu Yaozong. Decades before the other political and liberation theologies discussed below, Wu Yaozong and the Three-Self Patriotic Movement used Marxist social critiques to deconstruct imperialism and colonialism from within the Chinese Protestant church.[2] But rather than a full survey of political, liberation, and hope theologies in this chapter, I hope to highlight the major themes, conversation partners, and foundational works that undergird the hope theologies of the Latina feminist theologians engaged in the next chapter, Ivone Gebara and Nancy Pineda-Madrid.

While it may not have been the earliest discussions of political theology, the German post-war theological conversation on hope is significant. During Adolf Hitler's political rise and solidification of power in Germany, theologians were by and large silent. Most German Protestant churches and the Catholic church ignored the warning signs of the atrocities to come, with a few notable exceptions such as Karl Barth, Dietrich Bonhoeffer, and the Confessing Church. By the time the National Socialist Regime reached the height of its power, theologians and practitioners had little theological ground on which to stand against Hitler and his ideological policies. The absence of a robust political and theological engagement on the side of the interwar German churches and academies led to the inability of theology to provide any meaningful resistance against the Nazis. Werner G. Jeanrond, for example, writes that after the fall of the National Socialist Regime, the lack of theological grounding motivated German theologians to answer two questions: first, why was there no theology of resistance in the face of the Nazis? And, second, how can we talk about a loving God after the Holocaust? German theologies of the 1950s and 1960s fixated on these questions and began to

2. Kwok, "Postcolonial Intervention in Political Theology," 223–25.

probe other unjust political systems such as South African apartheid and dictatorial regimes in Latin America.

A second theological dialogue on hope we will explore in this chapter began to take shape in the mid-twentieth century Latin American context. Liberation theologians Leonardo Boff and Clodovis Boff argue that a contextual mix of socio-political, ecclesiological, and theological shifts in Latin America during the 1950s through the 1980s, formed "liberation theology."[3] German political theology's focus on hope was an understanding of the resurrection that called individuals to action. Specifically, the resurrection was a symbol of the future, which was not-yet-conscious, that functioned by shaping our present practices and political actions. Liberation theologians, such as Jon Sobrino and Ada Maria Isasi-Díaz on the other hand, place the community as the central player that enacts and embodies the hoped-for future.

A third strand of hope theologies can be found within the late twentieth-century context of the United States Catholic Church, where hope theologies were further complicated by the deep diversity of communities and contexts found there. Catholic theologians of this late twentieth and early twenty-first century era wrestled with understanding hope as a universal human experience, while acknowledging the importance of context in shaping hope. For Roger Haight and Elizabeth Johnson, the resurrection of Jesus Christ exemplifies and confirms hope, but is not exclusionary of non-Christians within communities of hope and their role in the embodiment of hope.

And finally, the fourth theological conversation on hope in our survey comes out of the same United States setting, but this conversation is even more contextually aware. Womanist theologians, situated within the African American community, argue for an understanding and practice of hope completely informed by communal contexts and shared narratives. The Black church and community ground this conversation, which is at the same time critical of the gender-blindness of many Black male theologians. Similarly, womanist theologians are in conversation with white feminists, but reject the idea of the universal woman's experience. In this way, hope must speak to the challenges and despair of both the legacies of racism and sexism for Black women in the United States.

Each of these theological expressions help to deepen the conversation on hope in light of its particular context. In conversation with and challenging the insights that came before, each of these conversations

---

3. See Boff and Boff, *Introducing Liberation Theology*, 66–77.

helps to complicate and nuance theology's engagement with hope based on their own contextual expressions of suffering. The survey of the twentieth and twenty-first centuries hope theologies below helps me to outline my own academic and personal contexts for this book, while also summarizing the major themes of Christian hope and clarifying what is at stake in this conversation around hope.

German Political Theologies of Hope

The overall anomaly of Germany during and after Hitler indelibly shaped political theological conversation. The full reality of what had happened, specifically the inability and indifference of Christians to speak against the tyrannical political system of Nazi Germany, set in over the decades following the end of WWII. German theologians, like theologians around the world before and after them, felt called to try and understand their situation. First, theologians both named and spoke out against the silence of the Church, pulling on narratives of the Christian Church as a political influence in this world, specifically pointing to Jesus' death as a political agitator against the Roman Empire.[4] The nature of the church, as the body of Christ, calls the Christian Church to speak truth into the political realm and hold "the political religions of our societies" accountable.[5] When theology fails to maintain a constant public dialogue around ethical action and the hopes for the future, we risk entering the conversation too late. Theologians of the post-war era argued that apathetic Christians allowed political situations to reach a point of no return. In reflecting on the German experience, Jürgen Moltmann names the problem as indifference. "Life was for us [Germans] a matter of indifference, because it had been made meaningless. We had stopped loving life so not to be so deeply touched by our own death and the death of people we loved. We wanted to make ourselves untouchable through an emotional armor of indifference."[6] Rather than indifference and apathy, our religious tradition calls us to dialogue and respond again and again, pulling from our roots as Christians in order to judge the ethical problems of our day and to hold our political systems accountable.

---

4. Moltmann, *The Experiment of Hope*, 110.

5. Moltmann, *The Experiment of Hope*, 111.

6. Moltmann, *Ethics of Hope*, 45.

The Christian theologians most central to shaping German political theology's conversation on hope are Jürgen Moltmann and Johann Baptist Metz. Moltmann and Metz are specifically concerned with what theology has to say in the political realm. Both theologians see theological hope as a call to action. The promised future, a future that is rooted in the actions of the present, calls Christians to live into that hope through social and political action. This call to action and resistance is in direct response to the silence and general apathy of the German church during World War II. In Moltmann's autobiography, he reflects on the concerns that he and others like Metz shared. He writes,

> At the deepest level, what led to the development of a political theology in those years was shock over the failure of the churches and the theologians in the face of the German crimes against humanity, symbolized by the name Auschwitz, a name that can never be blotted out. Why that appalling Christian silence?[7]

This question haunted German theologians and helped to frame their theological conversations, theology's role in the German political sphere, and the importance of hope in our Christian worldview.

Jürgen Moltmann and Ernst Bloch: Hope and the Not-Yet-Conscious

The writings of Jürgen Moltmann have, at times, dominated the conversation around theological hope throughout the second half of the twentieth century. At the age of sixteen, during the Second World War, the German Air Force drafted Moltmann, who then spent several years in prisoner of war camps throughout Europe. After this harrowing experience, in which he witnessed death and experienced suffering, Moltmann returned home to Germany to study theology and eventually received his doctorate. His theological questions were greatly shaped by his and the German people's experience of the rise and fall of the Nationalist Socialist Regime along with the relative impotence of the Christian Church in the face of evil, then and today. From the 1960s until the present day, Moltmann has been a prolific theological scholar, with several volumes dedicated to the topic of hope. His theology of hope is clearly shaped and influenced by German Marxist and Jewish philosopher, Ernst Bloch. Bloch, about thirty years Moltmann's senior and Jewish, experienced

---

7. Moltmann, *A Broad Place*, 156.

World War II from the other side. During the years of Nazi controlled Germany, Bloch lived as a refugee in several European countries and the United States. Also, during that time, Bloch wrote and published *The Principle of Hope*, his three-volume tome on hope, Marxist ethics, and utopianism. This work, by Bloch, helped shape Moltmann's own understanding of hope and we can see its influences throughout the Western European theological conversation on hope.

For Jürgen Moltmann, as well as his philosophical influence, Ernst Bloch, hope is a natural aspect of human existence. Both thinkers are heavily influenced by the German existentialist notion that anxiety, fueled by the human situation, is the central disposition of humanity. Humans, as incomplete creatures, live out their lives across a broad spectrum spanning hope and despair, where context, relationships, and other factors shape their response to their future-oriented reality.[8] Bloch, in the tradition of the existentialists, roots this anxiety and hope in the reality of our contingency—Because we are alive, we fear death and look to keep living. This reality is humanity's natural disposition towards hope. Moltmann follows this line of thinking as well, arguing that the human knowledge of our own precarious existence innately pulls us toward the future. Our will to survive and continue to exist into the future is what pulls humanity forward in time.[9]

Based on the idea that hope is a natural part of human life, both authors understand hope as a realistic endeavor. The reality of our human existence is that it is not static. As humans, we experience massive change, both individually and collectively, over the course of our existence, and we have a range of options in how we respond to change. Given humanity's

---

8. See Moltmann, *The Experiment of Hope*, 27 and 32.

9. Bloch looks at humanity's natural hope as tied to our self-preservation drive. Critiquing both Freud and Jung for only looking to the past for what drives human psychology, Bloch locates the most fundamental human drive in the future. Bloch writes that, "This drive is the self-preservation drive, it alone might be so fundamental – no matter what changes occur – as to set all the other drives in motion in the first place" (Bloch, *The Principle of Hope*, 64). Bloch points to the human drive to eat as one of the most central, even more basic than other drives outlined by psychoanalytics such as the sex and death drives. Moltmann and Bloch both tie this to humanity's future oriented reality. Hope in the future, rather than despair, pulls humanity forward in time as a natural drive. Moltmann points to examples of death and criminality as contrary examples that help prove this rule. Moltmann writes that "Both, death from expired hope and criminality from hopelessness, show that man, as a temporal creature, is directed toward the future and that this is a direction that alone corresponds to hope" (Moltmann, *The Experiment of Hope*, 22). Our natural orientation and submission to the future means that humanity is in essence open-ended.

ability for creativity, resilience, and ingenuity, it is as realistic to respond to our anxiety with hope as it is despair. Simply put, we should have hope, because the only thing we can know for sure is that things will change. Moltmann argues that this future horizon is completely open, which is the nature of hope, and this openness is the antithesis to depression and melancholy about the current state of life.[10] Because, the reality is, the current situation is not permanent, and we must always be concerned with the possibilities held in the openness of the future. Moltmann defines hope by this openness. "Hoping does not mean to have a number of hopes at one's disposal. It means, rather, hoping to be open."[11] In hope, humanity recognizes its nature as future-oriented and open-ended. In this same way, despair is not the loss of a few particular hoped-for events, but rather closing ourselves off from imagining a different and better future, and relinquishing our role in creating that future.

For both Moltmann and Bloch, our hoped-for future is both fully in the future and embedded in the present. Since the future is fully open, it is something that is not-yet-known, and yet in order to be understood it cannot be fully new, but rather must be based in our current world. Hope is a "venturing beyond." Rather than only considering the "In-Front-of-Us," Bloch talks about the "Not-Yet-Conscious," which is a fully unknown aspect of the future that is always in production. Bloch's driving purpose behind his work, *The Principle of Hope,* was to bring the Not-Yet-Consciousness of hope into words for philosophy to consider.[12] This aspect of hope for Bloch is what allows the truly novel to appear before us and keeps our future open. Moltmann ties this novelty of hope to God. We can have hope because God can bring something completely new into being.[13] Both Bloch and Moltmann ground hope in this possibility for "the new" because hope is only possible and meaningful when humanity has the power to change their circumstances.[14] Essentially, where there is no possibility for novelty, there is no hope. The novelty of the future, that we begin to understand as we move into the future, is always being surpassed by a new impossibility. This is one reason why novelty and hope are always context dependent. Moltmann writes, "that which appeared to one generation as 'ultimate' to be seen by a later generation as within

10. Moltmann, *The Experiment of Hope,* 16.

11. Moltmann, *The Experiment of Hope,* 20.

12. Bloch, *The Principle of Hope,* 7.

13. Moltmann, *Theology of Hope,* 30.

14. Moltmann, *Theology of Hope,* 92.

history and surpassable."[15] Hope is always being surpassed, giving way to a new impossible ultimate novelty projected into the future.

While hope is always "Not-Yet-Conscious," it is also always embedded in our present. Bloch explains this by collapsing time. We are able to see the seeds of future novelty in the once present, but this is only visible to us after we have moved into the future. It is only our own hindsight that reveals the roots of our hope.[16] Moltmann, on the other hand, understands this paradox through God's being. God, while present, is also ahead of us. God's being, existence, and communion is temporally defined as being into the future. If hope were not in some aspect in our present, we would be unable to anticipate the future. "We do not *extrapolate* the future out of the present; rather we *anticipate* the future in the present."[17] If we did not anticipate the future, our hope would be completely unknown and foreign to our understanding. This would cut us off from the possibility of that future and we would be unable to work towards its realization. This present embeddedness of hope takes on the form of a "promise." The promises of the hoped-for future are what drive us to practice imagination and embodiment of these hoped-for realities.[18]

Johann Metz and Karl Rahner: Solidaristic Hope

Johann Baptist Metz, a German Catholic theologian and contemporary to Moltmann, was also a central figure to the German political theological scene after World War II. With a surprisingly similar experience to Moltmann, Metz was also drafted into the German military as a young man, spending the final six months of the war in a prisoner of war camp in the United States. Returning to Germany, Metz completed a doctoral theology program under the tutelage of Karl Rahner at the University of Innsbruck. Metz remained a professor in the German academy until his death in 2019. Metz's mentor and major influence Karl Rahner's own academic training was heavily shaped by the presence and thinking of existentialist Martin Heidegger. Rahner finished his schooling at

15. Moltmann, *Theology of Hope*, 126.

16. Bloch, *The Principle of Hope*, 9.

17. Moltmann, *The Experiment of Hope*, 52. See also, Moltmann, *The Future of Hope*, 10.

18. Moltmann, *Theology of Hope*, 18.

Innsbruck and became a lecturer before the war when Nazis took over the University. During the war, Rahner taught and pastored in Vienna. After the war, he returned to Innsbruck. The influences of Heideggerian understandings of time and the future on both Metz and his academic mentor, Rahner, are significant for us to understand Metz' approach to Christian understandings of hope.

Rather than a linear understanding of time, where the future is understood as something fully new, coming directly after the present, Heidegger understood the future as the heart of the present and fully determining the present. Specifically, Heidegger places the event of death at the center of our existence. For Heidegger, the event of our death shapes our existential reality. This sentiment, that the future shapes the present in such an essential way, is central to both Rahner's and Metz's understandings of the future and the human person's connection to their future. To describe this influence on humanity, Rahner uses the word *Vorgiff*, which is a dynamic part of the spirit that reaches out beyond the self, labeling it a part of human nature. *Vorgiff* reaches out "towards the absolute range of all possible objects."[19] For Metz, this rejection of a progressive, linear understanding of time is important for a Christian worldview.

Metz argues that a horizontal and strict understanding of time as mono-directional, a mindset that he labels as an "evolutionistically shaped understanding of time," results in "the end of history and for the death of the person as a subject."[20] Rather, Metz, in the tradition of Heidegger and Rahner, believes Christian hope, as imminent expectation, shapes time. Hope, from the future, reaches back to us in the present and helps to sculpt our current worldview. Imminent expectation is the Christian hope of Christ's return and our call to discipleship in the present because of that immanence. Rather than a worldview that results in the erasure of God over time, or places the Kin-dom of God as a utopic linear end, Metz' understanding of the future and Christian hope is that it actively shapes the present through its own imminent expectation. Because the present is always preparing itself for the future, both are dependent upon each other and cannot be understood linearly.[21] Present and future are dialogically and relationally intertwined.

Metz argues that Christian hope does not promise a utopia that lies at the linear end of time, nor can we think through it to the point of

---

19. Rahner, *Hearer of the Word*, 47.

20. Metz, *Faith in History and Society*, 82.

21. See Metz, *Faith in History and Society*, 160–161.

full understanding. Rather, Christian hope is aware of the inescapability of death, which shapes our lives existentially. To ignore these realities would be irrational and undermine our Christian hope of imminent expectation. Rather, our deaths and the death of Christ become "dangerous memories," which influence the present, by problematizing the past in light of the expected future. If the past is "over and done with" as soon as it is past, we may imagine the future as fully new, and unconnected to the past or present. Metz roots this modern move in "secularization" or "evolutionistic thinking." Religion loses out to the primacy of the future in modern thought, unless it begins to embrace its own rootedness in the future, specifically in the promise, which holds us accountable to the losses and what has not yet been realized.

This dangerous memory is not meant to result in hopelessness, but rather spur us to a solidaristic hope, which is historically and socially mediated.[22] For Metz, solidaristic hope is the understanding and praxis of God's salvific power and promise for creation, at the heart of Christian faith and practice. This hope is not a selfish concern with salvation or the afterlife, but primarily concerned with others and the promise from God to raise the dead and bring about revolution on behalf of the forgotten, the lost, and those who suffer. This hope is not idle, rather it is a call to action and a deep invitation to engage life fully. "This hope does not paralyze historical initiatives or the struggle for all to be subjects. Rather, it guarantees the stability of those standards with which men and women, faced with the accumulated suffering of the just, stand up again and again against the prevailing unjust conditions."[23] Metz's solidaristic hope is not only an understanding of God's promise of salvation to all people, but is embodied by those who practice it within history and communities.

Metz labels the praxis of solidaristic hope "discipleship." In order to live into our call as disciples, our sense of imminent expectation should shape our understanding of hope, in that it should be practiced with haste and a sense of urgency. If we maintain our imminent expectation of God's promise, our discipleship will not fall into apathetic non-action or hatred.[24] Considering Metz's context of World War II Germany and the general apathy the Christian churches had in the face of the Third Reich, this message was a significant one. Unlike the apolitical, hands-off approach that the German churches had towards the rise of Nazism, Metz

22. Metz, *Faith in History and Society*, 169.

23. Metz, *Faith in History and Society*, 84.

24. Metz, *Faith in History and Society*, 163.

argues that Christian hope is not passive, but rather historical, social, political, and involved.

German Political Theology:
Resurrection Hope as Inspired Action

Moltmann and Metz's political theologies both ground our ethical praxis in an understanding of hope as projected into the future. Specifically, for both theologians, our hope for the promised future shapes our actions in the present and is understood through elements of the past. Ernst Bloch understands hope as having a dual role in calling us to action. First, we must reject that which leads to human oppression and suffering. Second, we must embrace that which leads to human flourishing in the future.[25] These two steps are key to the realization of our hoped-for future and the central action of political theology. They are also steps that appear in several other forms of liberation theology, such as mujerista and womanist theologies.

German political theology focused on hope as a motivator for action and resisting hate, rather than passive fear. For these thinkers, the biblical promise roots Christian hope. The promise of a utopian future we received from God in revelation and scripture motivates Christians to live into that hope. The future of freedom, peace, and justice haunts our present history and social imaginary. Hope in the becoming, the future promise of social reality, unsettles us and should energize us into action. The disconnection between our reality and that which God promises awaits us in the future won't let us rest. Instead of being complicit in the oppression and suffering of others, the mission of the church calls us to be a "constant disturbance in human society."[26] Living into a solidaristic hope, or taking political action is not an easy task. It is easier to focus on the present and our personal happiness and needs. It takes courage and a sense of selflessness to look prophetically into the future and discern the path in the present that leads towards all human flourishing. Eschatological promises are not meant to remain distant and unattainable, forever set in the future or after our deaths. And German political theology is most concerned with our call to live into these promises in the present. Our future hope calls us to action in our present moment. Moltmann

---

25. Bloch, *The Principle of Hope*, 75.
26. Moltmann, *Theology of Hope*, 22.

names the hopelessness and apathy that often plague us in face of such disconnected experiences, sin. He writes, "That is the sin which most profoundly threatens the believer. It is not the evil he does, but the good he does not do, not his misdeeds but his omissions, that accuse him. They accuse him of lack of hope."[27] Hopelessness, and apathy as a result, is the sin that continues to plague our society.

For both Metz and Moltmann, the narratives of the cross and resurrection of Jesus Christ root Christian hope. Jesus' teachings about the Kin-dom and the tradition of the resurrection both angle the Christian imagination towards the future and root Christian ethics in this future-oriented imagination. The resurrection and the cross are the central narratives of Christian's understanding of God's promise for the future. The resurrection is the subversion of the narrative of death, and the revelation of a future where God brings all of humanity, even the dead and defeated, back into flourishing. The resurrection is the eschatological promise that we are not forgotten. On the other hand, the cross, as the central symbol of human suffering, despair, loss and defeat, roots this promise in reality, past and present. The resurrection, divorced from the cross, would not only deny the reality of suffering, but it would be a completely new reality, unrelated to the past and therefore unimaginable. Rather the cross, paired with the resurrection, connects the not-yet-conscious with the present, creating a liberative and salvific narration of history.[28] The centrality of the cross and resurrection are significant for Christian hope because they signal the overcoming of suffering, death, and forgottenness.

Latin American Liberationist and Mujerista Theologies of Hope

The German political theology conversation overviewed above influenced many aspects of the twentieth century theological engagement around hope, especially within the academies of Europe and both the Protestant and Catholic churches during the mid-twentieth century. German political theology's early commitments, especially those of Karl Rahner, heavily shaped the focus of the Second Vatican Council of the Catholic Church, resulting in documents such as *Gaudium et Spes,* which brought the concerns of political theologians into the larger Catholic theological

27. Moltmann, *Theology of Hope*, 23.

28. Metz, *Faith in History and Society*, 89.

imagination. The second theological conversation around hope I engage in this survey began in Latin America during the socio-political precipice of the 50s and 60s. Following decades of revolutionary wars throughout the continent, many Latin American countries struggled for their independence, fighting the rise of dictatorial regimes, which were often backed by neo-colonial influences and strengthened by the global presence of ideologies such as fascism and communism. As Latin America struggled to become industrially developed, its countries were plundered by their own governments, the upper-class, and global partners for the natural resources of the region. This resulted in a majority, unsettled and impoverished class of the poor and oppressed.

During the colonial era and the first half of the twentieth century, the Catholic Church unfortunately played a role in supporting the ruling governments, through priests and bishops, who often benefited from such policies as members of the upper-class. This shifted in the 1960s as the Catholic Church began to awaken to its social mission and actively respond to political injustices around the world. In the wake of Vatican II, which stressed the Church's proper relationship with the larger global society, as well as encouraged greater freedom and creativity from both the clergy and laity, many Latin American theologians began to more deeply engage their specific contexts.[29] Liberation theology developed out of Latin American theologians' engagement with and response to the political, economic, and ecclesial changes taking place in Latin America throughout the twentieth century.

One watershed moment for the formation of liberation theology was in 1968, in the wake of Vatican II. The Latin American Episcopal Council (CELAM) met in Medellín, Columbia, producing several progressive documents with the specific aim of applying the call of Vatican II to the Latin American context. Alongside the larger Catholic institutional shifts, many theologians, clergy and laity, began to consider their specific cultural and political situations with an increasing awareness of unjust human suffering and the moral imperatives of gospel principles. One prominent Latin American theologian, Catholic priest, and advisor at Medellín, Gustavo Gutiérrez, broadened and advanced this new theo-ethical consciousness. In conversation with theologians such as Juan Luis Segundo, Hugo Assmann, and Lucio Gera, Gutiérrez called theologians and the Church to actively respond to the cries of the poor and suffering

---

29. See Boff and Boff, *Introducing Liberation Theology*, 66–77.

in Latin America. Gutiérrez coined this newly evolving and revolutionary brand of theology "liberation theology."[30]

Liberation theology is centrally concerned with the liberation of
the poor and oppressed. The object of hope in liberation theology is the
liberation of the community through complete solidarity and mutuality within the systems that shape it. This future liberated community,
made up of self-actualized individuals who live in interdependence and
solidarity, is a hope that pulls the present community forward and calls
them to a particular type of praxis. One way in which liberation theology's understanding of hope distinguishes itself from the German political theology conversation is in its focus on particular communities and
practices of solidarity. Since German political theology was responding
to a particular problem—the rise of Nazism and the relatively silent
church response—the reaction was a general call to denounce corrup-
tion and live into a hoped-for future. This vision of utopia shaped the
present deductively. On the other hand, throughout liberation theology's
formation the focus was more on the needs of the oppressed and poor,
inductively moving outward towards the imagined future. Over time,
this emphasis on a communal vision that empowers human beings and
radiates outward into society becomes even more centrally focused on
the lives of poor women. Later generations of feminist Latina and mujerista theologians address the lack of awareness around gender's role
in oppression and violence by the male liberation theologians, such as
Gustavo Gutiérrez and Jon Sobrino. So, while similar to German political
theology, liberation theology was contextually responding to the Latin
American systems of class inequality, deeply shaping the way liberation
theologians engaged hope.

Jon Sobrino:
A Hope against Hope Inspired by the Cross

Jon Sobrino is one of the major Catholic contributors and shapers of
Latin American liberation theology. Born in Barcelona, Spain in 1938,
Sobrino joined the Jesuits when he turned 18 years old and was sent to
El Salvador. The context of Latin America as well as the budding libera-
tion theologies of fellow priests such as Ignacio Ellacuría all shaped So-
brino. Ellacuría's own theologies of liberation were indebted to Spanish

30. See Berryman, *Liberation Theology.*

philosopher Xavier Zubiri, who critiqued the western philosophical separation between sensing and intelligence. Traveling some to the United States and Germany, Sobrino was also exposed to German political theologies. Sobrino returned to El Salvador where he was a major voice against the brutality of the Salvadoran Civil War. Sobrino, along with his other Jesuit brothers, spoke strongly against the violence and called for a quick end to the fighting that resulted in 75,000 deaths (a majority of which were civilians). This opposition caused the Jesuits to become targets for violence themselves, and in 1989, while Sobrino was out of the country, the Atlacatl Battalion of the El Salvador Army attacked and killed the six Jesuits in the household, including Ellacuría, as well as the housekeeper and her fifteen-year-old daughter. In light of this tragedy, Sobrino continued forward as a vocal advocate for peace and the poor in El Salvador. Consequently, Sobrino's formation in El Salvador deeply shaped his theological writings. The hope that Sobrino outlines in his works is a hope in response to a violent civil war and his experience of intimate loss.

Much of Sobrino's theological contributions focus on Christology, the life of Jesus, and particularly his mission of liberation. In this same vein, Sobrino's understanding of the cross roots his understanding of hope. Sobrino connected the cross and resurrection of Jesus with the Salvadoran people's own language about their experiences of life and death.[31] Sobrino turns to the context and experience of the marginalized, poor, and oppressed in his country of El Salvador using the term "crucified people," coined by Ignacio Ellacuría, a martyr and fellow Jesuit of El Salvador. Sobrino argues that this term, "crucified people," is more accurate than popular academic terms such as the "third world" or "the south," which scholars often use in conversations *about* the poor and oppressed around the globe.[32] The term, "crucified people," also exposes the nature of these communities' experiences of suffering. Which is to say, using cross language "expresses a type of death actively inflicted," revealing the injustice and systems of evils at work in the world today.[33] Sobrino continues, "And it is right to call them this because this language stresses their historical tragedy and their meaning for faith."[34] The "crucified

31. Sobrino, *Christ the Liberator*, 15.

32. Sobrino, *The Principle of Mercy*, 50.

33. Sobrino, *The Principle of Mercy*, 50.

34. Sobrino, *The Principle of Mercy*, 51.

people" act as a light to expose the true nature of our world and nations, revealing and naming the evils that often go ignored.

This turn to the "crucified people" as a location for hope and salvation renews the scandal of the cross. Sobrino believes this contextualization keeps the cross relevant and the "crucified people" of history become the "bearers of salvation," refusing to let the cross remain in the past.[35] Those that the world has rejected become its path to healing. Sobrino's interpretation of the significance of the cross and resurrection for hope differs from the German theologians in the previous section because Sobrino stresses that the resurrection as a symbol of hope is only significant because it is the resurrection of "the crucified one." The German hope theologians above stress the overcoming of death in the resurrection; the resurrection counteracts the cross by overturning death. But for Sobrino, there is a slight difference in his interpretation of the cross, which is a symbol that signals more than just death, but Jesus' rejection and persecution. Sobrino argues the "crucified people" of the world embody Christ in their practices of solidarity, service, simplicity, and readiness. For Sobrino and Ellacuría, the "crucified people" become living examples of hope against hope, through their struggle, resistance, and community.

Sobrino picks up Paul's language of Christian hope as a "hope against hope" (Rom 4:18). Sobrino balances between the despair of the cross and the optimism of the resurrection, opting for a resistance to both, which "arises out of the resurrection of the crucified one."[36] This connects hope to our lives and, in particular, the lives of the poor, which are situated in suffering and oppression, but contain the promise of resurrection. Hope in Jesus is a "qualified hope," a general openness to the future, and a precondition to understanding the resurrection.[37] This hope calls us to historical consciousness of the importance of praxis following the life of Jesus, who lived and died for the poor. Sobrino locates hope at the cross because it is the symbol of sacrificial utopian thinking that resists both death and oppression in faith of apocalyptic expectation. The significance of the cross as a symbol of Jesus' rejection, persecution, and sacrifice for Sobrino pushes the German hope theologies of Moltmann and Metz above and beyond the cross and resurrection as symbols of overcoming death. But rather, Sobrino interprets the cross and resurrection as signs of hope for all those who suffer and the world rejects.

35. Sobrino, *The Principle of Mercy*, 53.

36. Sobrino, *Christology at the Crossroad*, 233.

37. Sobrino, *Christology at the Crossroad*, 244.

This is not without critique. In their writings, Sobrino and Ellacuría try to distinguish between lifting the "crucified people" up as exemplars of hope and glorifying their suffering. This distinction is not always clear in their writings. Ellacuría does nuance this point more clearly at times, highlighting the importance of dialogue between both the death of Jesus and the "crucified people."[38] By keeping both Jesus' death and the "crucified people" in dialogue as sites of salvation, liberation theologians attempt an acceptable balance. Feminist liberation theologians revisit this issue more fully, continuing to critique the glorification of suffering and the language used by Sobrino and Ellacuría. Some of Sobrino's depictions of victims and perpetrators can be problematic when thinking about the issue of domestic violence. For example, Sobrino sees "crucified people" as exemplars of forgiveness.[39] Forgiveness is a fraught subject within the context of domestic violence and scholars should only approach this conversation with nuance and depth.

Aside from their living example, another way the "crucified people" of history provide hope is through practices of resurrection. Sobrino and Ellacuría call Christians to practice resurrection by bringing the "crucified people" down from the cross. One way Christians can practice resurrection and participate in salvation is through cultivating and witnessing the resurrections of the "crucified people," specifically working towards the end of their suffering.[40] Our responding and rising from crucifixion will look differently depending on the affliction. Resurrection, hope, and healing are not only shaped by their context but also the practices that work out salvation in the here and now. In his Christological text, *Christ the Liberator: A View from the Victims*, Sobrino argues that in the same way Jesus' cross can only make sense from within the contextual experiences of the "crucified people" of today, the resurrection is also only fully realized if the "crucified people" become "risen beings" in history.[41] Sobrino refers to these moments of hope, in which the "crucified people" become "risen beings" as "Easter Experiences."[42] If we are to understand Christian hope, we cannot remain disconnected from the reality of resurrection.

38. Ellacuría, "The Crucified People," 210.

39. Sobrino, *The Principle of Mercy*, 56.

40. Ellacuría, "The Crucified People," 223–24.

41. See Sobrino, *Christ the Liberator*, 14–15 and 74–76.

42. Sobrino, *Christ the Liberator*, 66.

At its core resurrection hope is not general but has, like Jesus' own ministry, a specific focus. Resurrection hope must be a hope oriented toward those who have been trampled down or left behind. Jesus was, himself, a victim of political violence, as well as a person who saw his mission as one directed toward the poor and oppressed of his day. This instinct to accompany and support those who suffer unjustly is subversive and dangerous work, particularly as it gives us a new awareness of all that must be changed in our social and political systems.[43] Our ability to access salvation and hope is at risk, if we fail to contextualize the cross and resurrection for our place and time. For this reason, Sobrino finds christologies that support a universal theology of hope inadequate. Specifically, Sobrino is skeptical of a hope that fails to be contextual or focused on the oppressed in our communities. Rather, Sobrino argues that Christology should both look to contextualize Jesus' life, teachings, death, and resurrection, as well as provide a specific contextual hope for the victimized of history.[44]

Ada María Isasi-Díaz:
Hope of *Proyecto Histórico*

Ada María Isasi-Díaz is another significant figure for us to engage in order to understand liberation theology's view of hope. Born in 1943, in Havana, Cuba, Isasi-Díaz came to the United States as a political refugee in 1960, where she entered the convent of the Order of St. Ursula. She spent much of her young adult years as a teacher or missionary in a number of places including Peru and the United States. It was in 1975, that Isasi-Díaz says she was "born a feminist" at the first Women's Ordination Conference in Detroit, Michigan. At that time, Isasi-Díaz began a deeper exploration of the intersection of race, gender, and class and took these questions with her through the rest of her university experience, receiving both an MA and PhD in theology from Union Theological Seminary by 1990. Isasi-Díaz coined the term *mujerista theology*, bringing liberation theology in close conversation with feminist theology and questions of economic class. The experience of Latina women, especially the poor and oppressed women within society, is the theological starting place for Isasi-Díaz's *mujerista* theology.

43. Sobrino, *Christ the Liberator*, 14.
44. Sobrino, *Christ the Liberator*, 12.

Similar to the liberation theology of Sobrino, Isasi-Díaz acknowledges that a religion that situates salvific hope in an unattainable future can further oppress the poor. Our glorification of self-sacrifice and promise of delayed rewards in the afterlife soothe the poor into accepting the status quo of their situation. With this in mind, Isasi-Díaz does not turn to the cross as her central symbol of hope, but rather develops an understanding of hope out of the community's experience, its ideal future, and its hope towards survival. Isasi-Díaz calls this hope the *proyecto histórico*, because it is the *historical project* that the community works towards constantly. The *proyecto histórico* refers to the Latina community's "liberation and the historical specifics needed to attain it."[45] When the community seeks to bring about the *proyecto histórico* as a reality it enacts its own liberation. But the community must also acknowledge that the fullness of that vision will not happen within history. Most importantly this hope is a two-part movement of denouncing and announcing, similar to Bloch's understanding of hope above. The community accomplishes the *proyecto histórico* by denouncing the oppressive structures and systems of sin, while announcing the hoped-for future in specifics. If we denounce the current situation without a goal in mind it is unhelpful and can lead us to apathy or fear. Both pieces, the analysis and denunciation of the present as well as the annunciation of the future are the core liberative praxis that make up *mujerista* theology for Isasi-Díaz. Her claim that *mujerista* theology is a liberative praxis itself "severely critiques and protests the diminishment of Latinas portrayed by the dominant culture, which does not recognize [Latinas] as intellectuals capable of critical and creative thinking."[46]

Outlined by Isasi-Díaz in her work *En La Lucha: A Hispanic Women's Liberation*, liberation has three aspects, which are specifically, 1) *libertad* (freedom), 2) *comunidad de fe* (faith community), and 3) *justicia* (justice). These three aspects in the present, happening simultaneously, drive our hope in the future.[47] Libertad is a psychological and social rejection of helplessness and dependence. It recognizes the importance of self-actualization and the need for individual and communal agency. The *comunidad de fe* is a social and spiritual acknowledgment of the interconnection and systemic nature of both our oppression and our liberation. The community of faith becomes a system that can replace the systems

45. Isasi-Díaz, *En la Lucha*, 34.
46. Isasi-Díaz, *En la Lucha*, 108.
47. Isasi-Díaz, *En La Lucha*, 37.

of sin that dominate the current context, providing individual support and community action enacting the *proyecto histórico*. *Justicia* is understanding solidarity as both a permission and a requirement within the community. To produce and promote a society that leads to human flourishing, regardless of race, class, gender, or sexual orientation, the entire community must allow all of its members to participate. Isasi-Díaz, like Sobrino, develops a hope theology that extends beyond the German hope theologians understanding of the cross and resurrection as symbols of overturning death. Isasi-Díaz's central concern is the significance of the cross and resurrection for the poor and oppressed: those who Sobrino calls "the crucified ones." Isasi-Diaz's focus on agency challenges and enhances the development of hope theology by accentuating the role of the whole community practicing hope and there by building and creating hope. The community participates not only in suffering but also in resistance, denunciation, restoration, and all other acts of resurrection, making hope an even more active and living communal reality. While the German theologians understand hope as a practice embodied on behalf of those suffering, and Sobrino argues that we practice hope in solidarity with the poor, Isasi-Díaz argues that the whole community must play their part in order to embody hope and move into the hoped-for future.

Liberation Theology:
A Communally Enacted Hope

Liberation theology's turn to the role of particular communities is significant for understanding hope as something that reaches beyond the individual and is enacted communally. Rather than a personal point of view, hope is culturally and collectively determined and embodied, taking on different significance and roles depending on the experience of the community. For both Sobrino and Isasi-Díaz, the community's central role in enacting hope connects it to salvation. For liberation theologians, the community is the key to salvation because of its ability to usher in healing and the promised future. Hope and salvation become explicitly related, in a way that was not directly communicated in the theological conversations of hope that took place in Germany in the first half of the twentieth century. Salvation is more than just the overcoming of death, which Moltmann and Metz stress as the significance of the cross and resurrection. The liberation theologians develop hope, in connection with salvation, as a healing of the whole community into the future.

For Sobrino, this communally determined hope continues to connect to the cross. In fact, Jesus' own resurrection was a communal experience. Sobrino, pulling from scripture, argues that Jesus' resurrection was not a solitary event but rather experienced by his whole community.[48] Sobrino unpacks the idea that the Jewish community of Jesus in Palestine would have understood itself in communal terms, similar to the indigenous roots of Latin American culture. The imagination of the disciples, shaped by a communally focused culture would have understood Jesus' resurrection as tied to the fate of their whole community. This collective mindset is one of the reasons why the resurrection provides hope, because it signals to everyone the communal experience of resurrection and liberation promised by God for all. Most importantly, the particular community Jesus aligned himself with during his life was the poor. Jesus' resurrection has particular meaning and promise for the poor, and calls all of us to be a church of the poor.

Isasi-Díaz connects salvific hope directly to the role of community in shaping ourselves, our imaginations, and working towards liberation. She writes, "For Latinas, salvation refers to having a relationship with God, a relationship that does not exist if we do not love our Neighbor. Our relationship with God affects all aspects of our lives, all human reality."[49] Isasi-Díaz argues that a Latina's relationship with God is as intimate, relatable, and daily as a relationship with a loved one. Our relationship with God is not only intimate but also inextricably tied to our communal relationships. Isasi-Díaz expresses this most clearly in her understanding of the *comunidad de fe*, which are communities of faith that reveal our interconnection to each other in both salvation and sin. Only communities that fulfill roles of support and action can be communities of salvific hope. Isasi-Díaz continues to outline that these communities, if they are communities of hope united by their struggle for liberation, are ecumenical and develop communal models of leadership.[50]

In summary, liberation theology shaped and deepened the theological conversation on hope, by including the role of the community as agents of hope. German political theologians, Metz and Moltmann, both argued that individual actions of social justice create hope for the future in the present. Sobrino and Isasi-Díaz deepen the embodiment

---

48. Sobrino, *No Salvation*, 106.

49. Isasi-Díaz, *En La Lucha*, 35.

50. Isasi-Díaz, *En La Lucha*, 41.

of hope in the present by moving beyond the individual's responsibility, to allow the community to help carry this burden. Pushing the German expression of hope theologies past the illusion of the individual, Latin American liberation theology argues the community as a whole can work to enact hope by creating a new imagined way of living in the world, one that they base on their knowledge of God's future promise of salvation. The whole community must practice hope or it will risk leaving aspects of the hoped-for future out of the conversation and reality that the community brings about.

Twenty-First-Century United States Catholic Theologies of Hope

The diversity of the North American context gives a particular grounding for theological conversations. During the latter half of the twentieth-century, the roles of race and gender in our everyday lived experience became a priority for theologies influenced by the civil rights movement. In the past decade, sexuality and sexual identification has joined the American conversation on identity and lived experience. Roger Haight talks about the concerns of the North American church as "four gifts" that we contribute to the Catholic church as a whole.[51] These gifts include religious liberty, the role of women, the role of the laity, and the role of other religions. The American constitution and the experience of living in America support each of these. These four gifts given by the American church to the world church, coupled with the significance placed on multiplicity and intersectionality within the twenty-first century American academy, have shaped and deepened the theological conversation around hope, specifically, bringing out the universal aspects of the hope-promise. Both Haight and Elizabeth Johnson understand hope in the same trajectory as Karl Rahner, as well as the political and liberation theologians engaged above, noting the present and future impact of God's promise to overcome sin and suffering. But, unlike German and Latin American theologians, Haight and Johnson expand hope to a universal human concern within communities regardless of the religious makeup of the community.

51. Haight, "Four Gifts of the American Church."

Roger Haight: Faith-Hope Rooted in Human Imagination

Roger Haight is an American Jesuit, who was born in 1936. Haight studied theology in the Philippines during the 1960s, finishing his education in the United States at the University of Chicago in the 1970s. He has taught theology at universities around the world, but is currently barred from teaching by the Congregation for the Doctrine of the Faith of the Catholic Church, because of his theological teachings about the nature of Jesus as a symbol, found in his book *Jesus: Symbol of God*. The influences of Karl Rahner and Vatican II, influences shared with Latin American liberation theologians, shape Haight's writing. Haight is clearly in conversation with both German political theologies and Latin American liberation theologies, as well as the North American concern with identity, such as issues of gender and race.

Haight's understanding of human nature roots his theological writings on hope. The fundamental aspects of our existence shape our human nature. Our existence and awareness of it creates a desire in us to continue to exist. It is a trust and a hope that we will continue into the future, which Haight calls "faith-hope."[52] Haight's connection of hope to our human nature does not make hope less significant or essential, but rather makes hope the "radical openness of the human spirit to being into the future."[53] Our human nature includes imagination, which uses faith-hope to envision possibilities for the future and take action to embody them in the present.

Haight also ties the Christian understanding of resurrection to the functioning of faith-hope. We have faith-hope that the human spirit will continue forward in our innate openness to the future, and the story of Jesus' resurrection symbolizes this. For Haight, humanity's creative side, our imagination, is what makes our faith-hope in Jesus' resurrection and our own resurrection possible.[54] Since our innate hope in continued existence grounds our faith-hope, our ability to have faith-hope in the future and our own resurrection precedes Jesus' resurrection and is not dependent on it in the same way that hope is dependent on the cross in the hope theologies discussed above. For German theologians, the cross and resurrection of Jesus are uniquely important to hope because it is the singular historical event that overcomes death. For Latin American

---

52. Haight, *Jesus: Symbol of God*, 141.

53. Haight, *Jesus: Symbol of God*, 347.

54. Haight, *Jesus: Symbol of God*, 125.

theologians, Jesus as "the crucified one," the one who rejected, is a singular representation of our ability to have hope. But for Haight, hope in our own resurrection was possible before the resurrection event of Jesus and comes from our human nature. For Haight, Jesus' resurrection is still significant and central to Christian theology because it is the full validation and realization of this faith-hope.[55]

The connection of faith-hope to both the resurrection of Jesus and our own promised resurrection, creates a relationship between faith-hope and our salvation for Haight. We do not just have faith-hope; we enact it.[56] By living into our faith-hope, through the enactment of our imagined future into the present, we are living into our salvific promise. This is most clearly seen in the disciples' reaction and understanding of Jesus as resurrected. The disciples' shift from despair to radical hope in Jesus' resurrection resulted in a new vision of reality and the realization of the salvific message of the resurrection.[57] But the salvific message of the resurrection is not an exclusive one to Christians, rather one that calls all within a community to embody hope.

Elizabeth Johnson:
Hope as Communal and Trinitarian

Elizabeth Johnson is a pioneering feminist theologian who currently teaches theology at Fordham University. Born in 1941, Johnson grew up as a member of a large Irish Catholic family in Brooklyn and as a young adult she joined the Sisters of Saint Joseph. In 1981, she was the first woman to receive her PhD in Theology from Catholic University of America, and continues to be a prominent scholar in the fields of feminist and Catholic theologies. Johnson's theology is also clearly rooted in Karl Rahner's understanding of Catholic theology, specifically his understanding of Christology and the role of context in understanding and engaging theology. Johnson is also influenced by both political and liberation theologies in the formation of her own feminist liberation theology.

While Johnson's understanding of theological hope influence much of her writings on feminist theology, we can find her most direct writings about hope in her book, *Friends of God and Prophets*. In this piece,

55. Haight, *Jesus: Symbol of God*, 141.
56. Haight, *Jesus: Symbol of God*, 151.
57. Haight, *Jesus: Symbol of God*, 348.

Johnson connects hope to communities in the present and to the communion of saints in the future. Johnson defines hope as "a firm expectation of something good to come, closely linked with the experience of yearning and desire for it."[58] In line with the tradition of the political theologies' and the liberation theologies' understanding of hope, Johnson ties hope to the tension between present reality and an expected future where God fulfills their promised glory. Johnson, like Rahner and Metz, grounds hope in a present realization of the not-yet-conscious and the promise of what is to come. Delving further into a systematic theology of hope, Johnson understands hope in light of the Trinity, through scriptural understandings of God's nature as creator, Jesus' resurrection, and the Catholic understanding of grace through the Holy Spirit.

Johnson also ties hope to communities, in a way similar to Isasi-Díaz's own commitments to the communal aspects of hope. Johnson argues that communities function around a shared hope for the future and the enactment of that hope in the present. This shared hope is what can create unity in communities of disparate peoples.[59] For communities, this hope vision also acts as an eschatological understanding for what lies in the future. The present is always going to shape this hope vision. The hoped-for vision must have some seed in the present shape of the community. Johnson pulls on Rahner's explanation of the future's connection to the present. The community's own self-narration of its relationship with God, through grace, shapes the possibility that lays ahead.

Both the present and future aspects of hope are further nuanced by Johnson as she ties the future envisioned hope to the communion of saints and the present enactment of hope in social justice.[60] For Johnson, the communion of saints is a similar symbol of future-promise to that of Jesus' resurrection, because it promises that there is more beyond destruction and death. The Christian tradition promises that death does not have the last word. We can see this promise in the Catholic understanding of the communion of saints. The communion of saints is a particular Catholic understanding of reality after we die. "Rather than persons being assimilated, mystically absorbed, or fused with the divine matrix, they will be quickened into new, inconceivable life in the communion of saints as God wipes away all tears."[61] For Johnson, with much left unrevealed,

---

58. Johnson, *Friends of God and Prophets*, 203.

59. Johnson, *Friends of God and Prophets*, 202.

60. Johnson, *Friends of God and Prophets*, 218.

61. Johnson, *Friends of God and Prophets*, 213.

what we *do* know about our experience after death and at the end of time is that all will be made well.

Similar to Haight's expansion of hope beyond the cross and resurrection, Johnson also increases hope by tying it to the symbol of the communion of saints. Hope develops in the present because of our connection beyond this reality through the Holy Spirit.[62] While Johnson builds much of her understanding of hope off the same theological reasoning as the other theologians in this chapter, Johnson's theological inquiry takes a unique path towards the inclusion of the communion of the saints in our experience of hope. Johnson's extension of hope to the communion of the saints further builds on the role of the community in practicing hope. As Latin American liberation theologians incorporate the historical community into their understanding of hope praxis, Johnson highlights the inclusion of a timeless community, pointing to a universal and eternal aspect of hope. As both the German and Latin American hope theologians focus primarily on the cross and resurrection and the roots of Christian hope, the incorporation of the communion of saints as a symbol of hope attempts to universalize hope beyond Christ, pointing instead to the role of the Holy Spirit. By connecting hope to the Holy Spirit in addition to Christ, non-Christians gain access to hope through their human nature.

Twenty-First-Century American Catholic Voices: Hope as a Universal Human Concern

For both Haight and Johnson hope is a future promise that impinges on present action. As with the German political theologians, we cannot completely untether the future from the present. The not-yet-conscious aspects of the future are familiar to us in the present or they would be completely unimaginable and unintelligible. This aspect of hope also calls us to enact hope, through social justice and present action. If our hope in the future is not embodied in the present, we lose our connection to that future and ultimately fail to enact its reality. Johnson expresses this notion through her explanation of the communion of saints. While the communion of saints anchors hope in the future eschatological promise, there is also an experience of that hope-promise coming into realization in the present. Johnson is sure to outline the significance of this hope for present action. She writes: "In light of the promised future, radical

62. Johnson, *Friends of God and Prophets*, 215.

hope then functions not as a lulling opiate but as a critical and creative power for the transformation of history in its personal, social, and cosmic dimensions."[63] Johnson uses the phrase "radical hope" here to signal the social justice call at the center of this type of hope. It is more than just an optimistic view of the future, but rather a radical call to change and work towards an imagined goal. This social justice component is central to being able to denounce present injustice and announce the hoped-for future, empowering those who struggle for justice, rather than trapping them in their present situation with the promise of a later reward.

Both Johnson and Haight connect Christian hope to God's promise that liberation will universally prevail over sin. Johnson understands this through her Trinitarian expression of hope. God promises to subvert sin in God's actions as Creator, the death and resurrection of Jesus Christ, and the present movement of the Spirit. God's promised and active love has been a universal presence through creation and history, as seen in the history of Israel and in Jesus, in Johnson's reading of scripture.[64] This universal aspect is also an important part of Haight's theology of hope. God's promise to remain active into the future in order to fully overcome all sin and suffering moves Haight to view this hope promise as one that affects all of creation, and not just Christians. "The Christian therefore is really sustained by hope in a promise, the promise of the resurrection, that the kingdom of God will be for all persons and for all of history. Given the doctrine of the universality of sin and the experience of it deep within the self, one cannot logically simply have hope only for oneself."[65] The twenty-first century American reality is the multiplicity of religions present within communities. For both Haight and Johnson, the universality of God's love extends the hope-promise to all within the community. The same Christian hope that calls us to social justice action, also calls us to a radical, neighborly love that envelopes all persons into our community.

This present community lives into the hope-promise for the future in the present, but that promise remains partially veiled. Johnson and Haight, track the promise of hope throughout scripture, history, and tradition, but this promise is far from being fully realized or revealed in the present. Johnson writes, "The Giver of life who created all beings out of nothing will still be there after final devastation, holding fast to the

63. Johnson, *Friends of God and Prophets*, 216.

64. Johnson, *Ask the Beasts*, 220.

65. Haight, *An Alternative Vision*, 255.

beloved creation. Without knowing particulars, these texts essentially declare the hope that the ultimate future will be blessed. Nothing more, but
also nothing less."[66] It is this promise, which Julian of Norwich repeats
when she says "all shall be well," that calls us to a faith-hope.

Twenty-First-Century United States Womanist Hope

Our context shapes hope and we always practice it in response to particular suffering, oppression, and violence. Womanists engage hope as one
possible response to the particular reality faced by Black women, which
in the United States has been shaped by the legacy of slavery, systems
of oppression, racism, and sexism. Hope appears in the works of many
womanist theologians as a mindset, attitude, and practice that directly
resists, protests, and points beyond the lived experience of oppression
for Black women. Also, like womanist theology as a field, concepts and
practices of hope are not monolithic; the ongoing dialogue among Black
women, contextualized by both their shifting circumstances and systems
of oppression, have shaped hope.

In her book, *Hope in the Holler: A Womanist Theology*, Elaine
Crawford argues that the suffering under slavery and slavery-inspired
institutions spurred a hope that was primarily concerned with this world,
the changing of oppressive systems, and daily survival. Tracing Black
theologies critique of German hope theologies, Crawford cites G. Clark
Chapmann, who argues that hope-theologies that focus on a too distant
future-based hope are unthinkable for persons who must fight for survival.[67] Chapmann argues that a future-directed hope may have been central
to the post-World War II Germans, like Moltmann, but when working
to navigate systems of oppression that in turn work constantly to destroy
you, Black communities in the United States look for hope and change
in the here and now. This doesn't mean womanist perspectives of hope
are not also concerned with the future promise and the King-om of God,
but rather womanist theologians are more centrally concerned with the
implications and meaning of hope for today in the face of the current
struggle for survival and flourishing.

One key historical context that has shaped womanist theologies of
hope is the North American slave trade. Womanist theologians wrestle

66. Johnson, *Ask the Beasts*, 221.
67. Crawford, *Hope in the Holler*, 4.

with the ongoing impact of slavery on Black people and the world. Whether you are considering the ante- or post-bellum United States, slavery has deeply scarred and shaped the experience of Black people. Womanist theologies of hope are integrally connected to Black women's experiences of slavery, post-slavery, and the civil-rights era. Even today, in a mythically "post-racial" society, the legacy of slavery is held in the bodies and systems of both Black and white persons. A hope informed by the context of slavery is unique and will naturally be different from a hope shaped under different circumstances. The oppressions experienced by African Americans is always shaped and connected to slavery. Even to-day, new forms of slavery, such as the school to prison pipeline for young Black men, systematically controls the bodies of people of color. Out of this experience of suffering, comes a particular conception of hope.

Black theologians and white feminist theologians struggled with "a similar single-vision analysis" understandings of hope.[68] Hope in white feminist theologies often centers around the experience of sexism for white women, while hope in Black theologies similarly center around the experience of racism for Black men. The discussion of hope within white feminism can be individualistic and blind to issues of race, while Black theologians' engagements with hope may ignore gender. For a hope that addresses Black women's concerns, we must address the concepts and practices of hope ignored by Black male and white feminist theologies. Because white feminist hope does not address issues of racism, it often leaves out the eschatological and soteriological aspects of hope that Black theology addresses. We must take into consideration the multifaceted nature of Black women's experience of oppression when exploring womanist perspectives of hope; the contextual nature of hope makes this imperative.

Womanist theological engagement with hope is also connected to a larger conversation on suffering and salvation. For womanist theologians, hope is the reversal of present suffering. Hope is the promise of a future that is significantly different from and in opposition to the present reality. In this way, the imagined hope, tied to both the future and salvation, functions eschatologically. While hope is a strong theme seen throughout the antebellum, postbellum, and civil rights era experiences of Black men and women in the United States, the way hope is engaged takes on a new theological focus during the early 1990s, as womanist

68. Crawford, *Hope in the Holler,* 5.

academics begin to articulate suffering and salvation for Black women. Delores Williams was one of the first womanist theologians to look at the cross and atonement through the experiences of Black women. For the theologians above, the cross and the resurrection were often sites of hope. This is problematic for Williams who troubles the cross in light of the surrogacy practices Black women experienced throughout history, choosing to locate salvation in the "wilderness experience" rather than the cross. Within the dialogue of womanist theology, many pushed back against Williams' rejection of the cross, and womanist theologians like JoAnne Marie Terrell worked to understand the cross and its significance for African Americans. Up to this point, the womanist conversation addressed questions of salvation, healing, and eschatology, all of which were non-direct ways of engaging and understanding hope. By the turn of the century, womanist theologians such as M. Shawn Copeland and Elaine Crawford began to directly engage hope in light of both the womanist theological conversation previous and the particular experiences of suffering and oppression uncovered in the lives of Black people.

M. Shawn Copeland:
Hope as Enfleshed Freedom

M. Shawn Copeland is a Catholic womanist theologian, who was born in 1947 and grew up in Detroit, Michigan. She studied systematic theology at Boston College, graduating with her PhD in 1991. Copeland has taught at a number of universities across the United States, including Xavier University of Louisiana, Yale Divinity School, and Marquette University. She recently retired from the Department of Theology at Boston College in 2019. Copeland was the first African American and first African American woman to hold the presidency of the Catholic Theological Society of America and also served as the convener of the Black Catholic Theological Symposium. Her career has focused on carving out academic and pastoral spaces for the African American community (especially women) in the Catholic world.

For Copeland, the cross is not a symbol of suffering alone, disconnected from other symbols of hope. In her book, exploring both theological anthropology and Christology in light of the bodily experiences of Black women, *Enfleshing Freedom*, Copland re-imagines Jesus' suffering body on the cross as not only connected to all bodies of suffering, but also the resurrection and the Eucharist. Copeland equates the body of Jesus with the bodies of Black women and puts both at the center of her theological thinking. For Copeland, the body is the central site of divine revelation because it so completely shapes our existence and social realities. The multiplicity of human bodies (race, gender, sexuality) and our nature as social creatures are unique windows to frame the divine as communal—specifically existing in multiplicity and solidarity. Copeland chooses to privilege the Black woman's body in order to make her theological exploration "specific and particular."[69] By making her theological claims about the cross and salvation specific and particular, rather than mistakenly universal, she brings all other particulars (regardless of gender, race, sexuality) into the body of Christ as well. Copeland asks, if Christ's body can't be understood as the body of a Black woman, then what hope does anyone have?[70] Copeland writes that connecting the Black woman's body and Christ's body in this way "lays bare both the human capacity for inhumanity and the divine capacity for love."[71] We uncover this through remembering the suffering and oppression experienced by both Black women and Jesus, as well as the memory of the resurrection.

Copeland sees hope in the experience of Black women who even in the midst of suffering and oppression worked towards survival and healing. Without covering over the evil perpetrated or glorifying their suffering, Copeland critically delves into the experience of Black women in the United States to find their traditions of resistance as symbols of the strength of human hope. Specifically, Copeland highlights Black women's oppositional uses of "word (sass) and deed (fighting back, literal escape)."[72] Copeland equates their resistance with the presence of the resurrected Jesus. Jesus who suffered, died, and resisted through resurrection becomes the ultimate symbol of hope for Black women who experience suffering and life-threatening oppression. Acknowledging the possible dangers that Delores Williams brought to light in her turning away from the cross as a symbol for Black women, Copeland embraces the cross because it is also the symbol of the Risen Lord, a symbol of resistance. The resurrection only connects to Black bodies if the body of Christ also experienced rejection.

69. Copeland, *Enfleshing Freedom*, 2.
70. Copeland, *Enfleshing Freedom*, 5.
71. Copeland, *Enfleshing Freedom*, 1.
72. Copeland, *Enfleshing Freedom*, 3–4.

The conclusion of Copeland's book focuses on the ability for the Eucharist to transform our bodies as the body of Christ, and most significantly makes our eschatological hope real and present in humanity. The Eucharist becomes the ultimate image of our faith in resurrection and our future hope.[73] The Eucharist unites all bodies in total solidarity, through the transformation of all those who consume the body of Christ. The Eucharist, by its nature, is in opposition to racism, which is lethal and divisive to bodies. Racism and white-supremacy are idolatrous, because they threaten the communion the Eucharist mediates and the solidarity that is central to orienting ourselves in the image of Jesus. For Copeland, the ability to practice solidarity is the heart of the Christian message and how we are to be in relation with God and each other. When practiced in true solidarity the Eucharist is salvific in that it "re-orders us, re-members us, restores us, and makes us one."[74]

Copeland understands the Eucharist as a subversive memory, that does not allow the forgetting or ignoring of the reality of bodily suffering. The Eucharist is not a bloodless, pristine ritual that covers over the reality of Jesus' life and death, but rather "the Eucharist memorializes the death of Jesus in a 'first century lynching.'"[75] The practice of Eucharist ensures that we do not forget the dangerous and subversive aspects of Jesus' cross and resurrection, along with the deaths and oppression of all those who are also represented on the cross. We can link the suffering of all to the cross that we can also link to the resurrection, which is the enfleshed freedom promised by God.[76] Eucharist, as a sacrament, creates solidarity among Christians, a solidarity that embraces all bodies regardless of marginalization. One of the most "dangerous" aspects of the memory of the cross and resurrection represented in the Eucharist is the universality of the hoped-for promise of freedom.

Eucharist as a symbol of solidarity is a call to action and specifically, for Copeland, a call to discipleship. Eucharist is a living memory that makes demands of us and our bodies as Christians. Similar to the theologies of hope rooted in German political theology, Copeland's understanding of hope in the Eucharist is an embodied practice, something we must live out in the present in order to bring about a promised future.

---

73. Copeland, *Enfleshing Freedom*, 107.

74. Copeland, *Enfleshing Freedom*, 128.

75. Copeland, *Enfleshing Freedom*, 110.

76. Copeland, *Enfleshing Freedom*, 124.

This hope shapes action, imagination, and our bodies. Copeland's rooting of hope in the resurrection, the Eucharist, and solidarity of the Eucharist meal, imagines a hope that is creative, open to the future, and committed to the work of liberation. This hope is the enfleshment of freedom, in that it embodies and brings about a hoped-for future that liberates Black men and women. For Copeland, hope is an act of resistance against present oppression, informed by the voices and experiences of Black women and their communities.

Elaine Crawford:
Hope as Contextually Dependent

Reverend Dr. Elaine Crawford is a United Methodist pastor in Georgia. Born in Indianapolis, Crawford was the first African American woman to earn a PhD in Historical Theology from Union Theological Seminary in Richmond, Virginia. She has held several university teaching positions in theology in addition to a career as a public preacher and pastor. Her work and writings have focused on creating pastoral spaces and resources for African American women and communities. While hope has always been an important part of Black women's survival strategy, Crawford argues for a resurgence in womanist theology's concern with hope in order to push Black women's liberation and empowerment forward.

Hope allows for both protest and empowerment for Black women. In her book, *Hope in the Holler,* Crawford tracks the connection between womanist hope and a practice of resistance against suffering, represented in "the Holler." Crawford unpacks her own meaning of Holler, writing that the "Holler is a primal cry of pain, abuse, violence, separation. . . The Holler is the refusal to be silenced in a world that denied their very existence as women."[77] The Holler, as a cry of resistance, is the root of African American women's hope since the time of slavery. As a subversive refusal to give up hope that life can and should be other than it is. It is an audacious cry that says "no" to the status quo of oppression and violence, while also hinting towards a hope based on "their passion for the possible in their lives."[78] Crawford does not separate womanist hope from the hol-

---

77. Crawford, *Hope in the Holler,* xii.
78. Crawford, *Hope in the Holler,* xii.

ler, but rather these two paradoxically create each other; she writes "it is Hope in spite of and in the midst of the Holler."[79]

Black women's hope for Crawford is the opposite of their oppression. Crawford understands womanist hope as specifically responsive to the particularity of Black women's suffering as 1) maldistributed, 2) enormous, and 3) non-catastrophic.[80] Hope must be particular or it cannot function as hope in order to overcome suffering, oppression, and violence. Black oppression is maldistributed, meaning that it is a suffering unequally experienced by humanity, but rather is an experience of oppression uniquely experienced by Black men and women. Therefore, womanist hope must also be maldistributed, or abundantly present, in favor of Black men and women. Black oppression is also enormous, fully eclipsing the individual's full potential of life, and fully life-threatening, therefore womanist hope must also be enormous, empowering all aspects of life for Black people. Finally, Black oppression is non-catastrophic, rather it is drawn out overtime—over lifetimes—meaning womanist hope must also be transgenerational. The Hope-Holler described by Crawford is a hope that comes directly out of particular experiences of Black oppression. Black women's hope has been shaped as a direct response to the suffering and violence experienced throughout their lives and the lives of their ancestors.

Twenty-First-Century Womanist Hope: Communal Narratives

Womanist theologies of hope further complicate and texturize our engagement with hope in this book. Specifically, womanist theologians unyieldingly root hope in particular contexts. We can not talk about hope unless it is in specific and particular terms. In line with Black theologians' argument that salvation has to be understood as a salvation within history, womanists understand hope to be less concerned with other-worldly hope than a hope that looks towards the changing reality of *this* world.[81] While the promise of the coming Kin-dom of God is important, the bringing about of that Kin-dom here on earth is of central concern for

---

79. Crawford, *Hope in the Holler*, xii.

80. See Crawford, *Hope in the Holler*, 17. See also Jones, "Theodicy," 28–38.

81. Crawford, *Hope in the Holler*, 103.

womanist theologians. Black women's hope is a radical hope that seeks change in the current world.

Womanist hope is understood as a counterpoint to Black women's oppression; womanist theologians understand suffering and hope as situated and particular to experience. In order to uncover the theological source of experiences for a historically oppressed group, methodologies of recovering and remembering are vital. The lives, narratives, and voices of Black women throughout history shape and mold womanist hope. Many womanist theologians turn to the voices of Black women in literature, biographies, and ethnographic studies. Up to the publication of her own book in 2002, Crawford's biggest critique of womanist theology's methodology was that it had not sufficiently listened to Black women's voices. Crawford believes that through the mining of Black women's voices in all eras, one can more fully uncover womanist understandings of hope. One way womanist theologians uncover these narratives is through qualitative research methods of remembering and recovering. Specifically, locating and analyzing the memories, stories, and accounts of Black women's hope.

Throughout history, memories and narratives have enacted hope in their retellings for communities of Black women. M. Shawn Copeland, in her chapter, "Wading Through Many Sorrows," argues that through the retelling of narratives and memories, enslaved communities resisted their current circumstances of death-dealing oppression. Through narrative and memory, enslaved communities could subvert the system of slavery within themselves, resisting the colonized-mind. This also leads to the embodiment of these narratives and practices of resistance.[82] While the context of Black women in the United States has shifted, it is not completely unfamiliar to daily realities of enslaved Black women. These narratives help to give language to modern day oppression and responsive hope.

By examining Black women's narratives, womanist theologians like Copeland and Crawford have uncovered an embodied and action based hope. Throughout all the oppressive eras Black people have endured in the United States, from slavery to the civil rights era to the current myth of the post-racial society, there has been evidence of a hope that is resistant and action based.[83] Crawford argues that the hope for a different

---

82. Copeland, "Wading Through Many Sorrows," 121.

83. Crawford, *Hope in the Holler,* xv.

future drives Black women's actions. Hope that the future could be different was fuel for their actions of resistance and shaped the type of practices they embodied. "Hope functions as a bridge between oppression
and liberation."[84] The Black community and the Black church ground
womanist theology, which often differentiates itself from white-feminism
in its refusal to walk away from its larger community. Black women have
experienced and practiced hope within communities of women, men,
and children from the time of slavery. The Black church, the Black family,
and the Black community, while not without problems for Black women,
have been integral to the womanist narrative.[85]

Womanist hope is specific and particular to Black women's experience in the United States. But this specificity does not exclude the wisdom
and insights womanists uncover about hope from our conversation about
hope after domestic violence. Hope, in direct response with a context of
suffering and the reversal of that context, will subvert the systems of power and control at the heart of domestic violence. As we will explore more
in the next chapter, domestic violence is a specific and particular context
that requires a similarly distinct re-imagining and practice of hope.

Theological Understandings of Hope Today:
Discerning, Holistic, Inclusive Action

Since the early Christians' first revelations of the resurrection of Jesus,
communities and their contexts have shaped Christian theology's understandings of hope. The earliest Christian communities experienced the
resurrection as a promise to humanity, informed by the innate understanding of the incompleteness of our human experience. This promise
was that evil and suffering had no place in our lives and God called us to
work towards a future that limited them. Throughout history, our understanding of evil and suffering have been culturally shaped and therefore
the future that we project is also determined by our cultural, historical,
and psychological contexts. Current theological conversations on hope
are deeply rooted in our current context—a context that has been shaped
by two world wars, the global rise of dictatorial regimes (fascist, com-
munist, and religious fundamentalist), globalism, a technological age,

84. Crawford, *Hope in the Holler,* 112.

85. See Williams, "Womanist Theology," 121, and Coleman, *Making A Way Out of
No Way,* 100.

a global ecological crisis, pandemic, and the increase in awareness and clashes over civil rights. The historical survey of hope theologies in the twentieth and twenty-first centuries contained in this chapter, situates the larger theological conversation of hope, and develops a larger cultural framework for understanding hope. Based on the discussion above and the trajectory of hope theology, hope takes on a particular meaning and shape as a *discerning, holistic,* and *inclusive* practice.

Discerning Hope:
A Future Image and a Present Action

We can understand hope as a part of humanity's ability to imagine our own futures. This imagined-future shapes our understanding of the present and calls us to live differently in order to move ourselves closer to that hoped-for reality. Bloch writes: "The work of this emotion [hope] requires people who throw themselves actively into what is becoming, to which they themselves belong."[86] Our ability to hope reveals our own sense of incompleteness in our present reality. Our lived experience becomes an authority by which to challenge the status quo, a revelation that can be an unwelcome idea to those who have benefited from the status quo. In this sense, hope is two-fold. Hope simultaneously calls us to action that is meant to bring about a hoped-for future, while also calling us to reject all aspects of our current reality that do not belong to or quicken that imagined future.

Hope is a prophetic two-fold action, including a denouncing of present suffering and evil along with the announcement of the promised future. We can see this theme of denouncing and announcing throughout all four conversations around hope outlined above and is central to our ability to enact hope. In Bloch's writing on hope's innate and evolutionary aspects, he talks about denouncing and announcing using "no" and "yes" language. Hunger drives humanity to sustain itself, by prompting us to hope for a future in which we are no longer hungry. We denounce our current hunger and announce our state of non-hunger that lies in the future. This two-fold thought process behind our hope, pushes us to action in order to subvert the present and enact the future. Moltmann, heavily influenced by Bloch's philosophies, also understands the future's effect on the present in this way. The hoped-for future, the promise, announces

86. Bloch, *The Principle of Hope*, 3.

itself and subverts the present. Moltmann writes, echoing Bloch's understanding of hunger, "In the promises, the hidden future already announces itself and exerts its influence on the present through the hope it awakens."[87]

This idea is explicitly outlined by liberation theologian Ada María Isasi-Díaz in her description of *Proyecto Histórico*, which includes these two movements. In the struggle for the promised future, God calls us to denounce present evil, which keeps us from realizing our hope, and announce the hoped-for future. This theme is found again in the theologies of hope found in Catholic American theologians, specifically the thought of Elizabeth Johnson. In rejecting a hope promise that encourages the complacency of the poor and oppressed, Johnson argues that hope is a radical and powerful force resulting in revolutionary action. And again, we see this theme in the writing of womanist theologians of the twenty-first century. In her investigation of Black women's narratives, Crawford finds women include both an account of the oppressive experiences that shape their lives as well as a deep faith in the hope-promise from God. These narratives become acts of resistance, by naming the evils of slavery, racism, and oppression while also holding onto a hope that things can be different; these women reclaim their personhood from the systemic dehumanization of their lived experiences.

Holistic Hope:
Individually and Communally Embodied

Similarly, as imagined-futures shape our present, that same hope shapes our daily actions both individually and communally. We embody the two-fold prophetic action of hope at an individual level as well as a communal level. For the German political theologians, in the cultural context of Germany after World War II, individual action and resistance was crucial. Christians inspired by hope could not remain sidelined. For Moltmann, hope transformed individuals towards action, not apathy.[88] Moltmann does not use "communal language" when talking about hope-action. The closest his writing comes to discussing communal actions of hope is in discussing the Christian Church as a body of influence in

---

87. Moltmann, *Theology of Hope*, 18.

88. Moltmann, *Theology of Hope*, 33. My emphasis.

human society.[89] Metz, on the other hand, has an understanding of "solidaristic hope," which brings the communal aspect of hope's embodiment into his theology. For Metz, individuals practice hope and hope-action on the behalf of others and publicly within society.[90] The public nature of individual actions we find within Metz's understanding of solidaristic hope isn't the same as hope being embodied communally, but hints towards the role of communities.

We can see the development of action rooted in hope as explicitly communal within liberation theology's conversation on hope. Sobrino clearly understands the resurrection as a communal revelation and without the community's acceptance and embodiment of this resurrection hope, Jesus' resurrection is not continually revealed. The community of the poor is the most significant because Jesus chose to align himself with them during his life. The communal embodiment of hope is also present in Isasi-Díaz's concept of *comunidad de fe*, which not only serves the purpose of enacting an alternate reality to systems of sin, but also functions as a system of personal support and community action. The hope of the community expressed in the *proyecto historico* determines the formation and actions of the *comunidad de fe*. Action in response to hope is always communally and culturally determined.

This conversation on hope's individual and communal aspects is further extended by Johnson, as she ties the community's function into the future to the communion of saints. The future reality of the communion of the saints, which is one of the causes of our present hope, reveals the indecipherable and eternal relationship between individual actions and communal actions of hope. Johnson argues that, "Finding expression in a community's imagery, rituals, and stories, [hope] arises in individuals insofar as they partake of this social reality."[91] We cannot separate the individual and community from each other. Johnson works to overcome the separation between individuals and communities, reminding us that we cannot have one without the other. Womanist theologians trouble this false-dichotomy even further. Pulling from the narratives of African American women during and after slavery, Crawford notes that these narratives "transcend preoccupation with individualism."[92] This a preoc-

---

89. Moltmann, *Theology of Hope*, 22.

90. Metz, *Faith in History and Society*, 84.

91. Johnson, *Friends of God and Prophets*, 218.

92. Crawford, *Hope in the Holler*, 27.

cupation that Crawford critiques in white feminist's writing on hope. But, in order for hope to be holistic, hope must be practiced both by individuals and in community.

Inclusive Hope: Revealed in
the Resurrection and as a Universal Human Concern

While Christian hope has often been connected to the cross and resurrection of Jesus, the relationship between Jesus' death, resurrection, and our hope for a promised future has shifted and deepened within the theological conversation around hope. For Moltmann, Metz, and Sobrino, the centrality of the cross and resurrection in situating Christian hope is clear. It is not until more recently in the plural context of the United States and a globalizing world that the conversation about Christian hope has become concerned with the universal and cosmic natures of hope, the cross, and resurrection.

Moltmann and Sobrino both spend much of their writing on hope connecting the cross and resurrection intimately together. It is the resurrection of the crucified one, the one who lost fully and completely, that gives us hope in our own salvation. The past resurrection of Jesus offers the promise of a future event that changes the reality of the cross and has consequences for our actions in the present.[93] Sobrino understands we do not base our hope on the cross or the resurrection alone, but rather it is because the resurrected one was also the crucified one that we can have hope. "If the cross of Jesus does not put an end to hope, then we have been given something that cannot be torn away from us (Rom 8:31–39)."[94] Tradition reveals that the cross is the root of our hope in as much as it is properly grounded in the resurrection event. Both the cross and resurrection shape the significance of each other and are incoherent separately. For Moltmann and Sobrino, the cross and resurrection inform each other and are the basis of Christian hope.

Metz, still connecting to the cross, broadens humanity's seed of hope, understanding hope as tied to memories of subversion, what he terms "dangerous memories." These memories include events such as the exodus and the resurrection, both instances when God subverted the earthly powers to reveal God's intentions for humanity. Memories of

93. Moltmann, *Theology of Hope*, 21.
94. Sobrino, *Christology at the Crossroads*, 232.

promise root Christianity's hope and determine how Christians live in the world.[95] Dangerous memories refer to the past but point towards the future promise, and both their memory and promise have weight in the present world. Similar to Moltmann and Sobrino's understanding of the cross and resurrection, Metz argues that we cannot disconnect our hope for the future from the events of the past, because the past deeply shapes them.

Womanist theologians further develop the contextual nature of hope. The cross and resurrection do not ground hope and hope practices alone. In fact, contextually based hope means that the types of action and embodiment that expresses hope in the lives of Black women has changed and adapted over time. "As the sociohistorical context of black women changed, so did the function, expression, and embodiment of hope."[96] For example, Crawford looked at the actions of slave women, who were cultivating their own sense of freedom, humanity, and voice through the telling of their life's journey. For slave women, hope was not just talked about, but embodied in their actions of resistance and survival. While these practices may have been simply ways of surviving, these actions were radical in their ability to transform the practitioners.

Broadening the conversation on hope to include the possibility of hope for other religions beyond Christianity, Roger Haight understands hope as a universalized experience. Haight argues that faith-hope is an innate trait to humans. The existential contingency of our human nature results in the necessity that we hope for the future in order to continue living.[97] As Bloch argued earlier, many of our basic instincts to sustain ourselves are acts of hope. Haight makes the case that therefore the cross and resurrection of Jesus are not the root of our Christian hope, but rather they are the particular fulfillment of our hope. Similarly, Johnson's work on hope theology expands Christian hope to the role of the Holy Spirit in symbols like the communion of saints. The universalizing of hope beyond Christ is a significant deepening of the hope conversation. Hope and its call to embody the promised future has no borders and can help to create a community that is ever more inclusive.

---

95. Metz, *Faith in History and Society*, 182.

96. Crawford, *Hope in the Holler*, 1.

97. Haight, *Jesus: Symbol of God*, 141.

Concluding Thoughts and Looking Ahead

To conclude, a variety of contexts throughout history have shaped the theological understanding of hope this book engages. While these conversations on hope continue to deepen each other today, overlapping and pushing against one another, several themes and definitions of hope come to the fore to inform our understanding of hope for this book. Hope involves a subversive call to dual-action, which both moves us to work towards an imagined future, while also rejecting all aspects of the present that are not life giving. Hope is both communally and individually realized and embodied, because as individuals we cannot flourish outside a life-affirming community and our communities cannot function without individuals who share an imagined future. And finally, hope is universal, as well as particularly expressed in the cross and resurrection of Jesus, pushing us towards a more and more inclusive vision of the future. Simply put, theological hope is a discerning, holistic, inclusive embodiment of God's promise for our lives.

Now that we have a foundational understanding of the major themes and components of theological hope, in the next chapters we will begin the particular work of contextualizing and exploring hope after domestic violence. First, I will narrate the socio-historical context and religious response surrounding the modern context of domestic violence in the United States. I intend this narration to help ground us in a particular context and community in our following investigations into hope. Next, we will name the particular crosses and resurrections of women in general, turning to the theological writings of Ivone Gebara and Nancy Pineda-Madrid for guidance. In dialogue with Gebara and Pineda-Madrid, we investigate a woman and trauma-centric resurrection narrative of the Empty Tomb, found in the Gospel of Mark, for insights into women's salvation and resurrection post-trauma.

2

A Brief History of
Domestic Violence and Theology

"The study of psychological trauma does not languish for lack of interest.
Rather, the subject provokes such intense controversy that it periodically
becomes anathema. The study of psychological trauma has repeatedly
led into realms of the unthinkable and foundered on fundamental
questions of belief."

—JUDITH HERMAN[1]

WE ARE IN A moment of public awareness around trauma, abuse, violence, and suffering. But, as Judith Herman reminds us, that awareness is fragile. The statistical reality of domestic and sexual abuse is shocking. The lack of public response is appalling. And the silence of the Church is unforgivable. These unpleasant and disturbing realities grate against our beliefs about ourselves, our world, our religious communities, and God. The theological questions, posed by survivors of domestic violence through the tinny phone receiver of an anonymous crisis line, still ring in my ear: Where was God when my husband attacked me and my children? Why do I have to bear this cross alone? How do I break my vow of marriage and leave? Who can I trust not to judge me? These are the questions that shatter our accepted theological worldviews. How do we— as theologians, as church leaders, as Christians— wrestle with these questions,

1. Herman, *Trauma and Recovery*, 7

stare into the reality of domestic violence, and not break? History shows us that it is easier to just turn away. But, if we are not going to turn away, we must hold our communities and theologies accountable, by surveying the historical relationship between religion and domestic violence and point to new ways forward.

In this chapter, I begin that survey by looking at the bodily, communal, and mental effects of domestic violence and how it shapes a person's ability to have and practice hope. Summarizing the conversation around domestic violence in the field of theology, this chapter begins with an overview of the problem of domestic violence and theology's engagement with domestic abuse. After a statistical and systemic overview of the issue of domestic violence itself, this chapter gives an ecumenical outline of the church's historical engagement with domestic violence, exploring both church documents and public stances on relationships, marriage, and family, highlighting the church's lack of direct response and engagement with this issue. Next, this chapter gives a summary of early feminist scholarship, engaging theologians such as Rosemary Radford Reuther and Marie Fortune, who worked to diagnose domestic violence as a theological issue. This chapter also describes the influences of trauma theologians to the theological conversation around domestic violence. My goal in this chapter is to argue the importance of moving the church and theologians' responses to domestic violence forward, beyond clergy and pastoral education and towards active community engagement.

Domestic Violence:
A Social and Psychological Overview

"A man's home is his castle; rarely is it understood that the same home may be a prison for women and children."

JUDITH HERMAN[2]

Throughout most (if not all) of history, women have struggled against policies and institutions of inequality based on their gender. Domestic violence is one such institution that haunts women's right to life and happiness. Using tactics such as physical violence, threats of violence, mind games, insults, minimizing, isolation, economic control, threats to loved ones or pets, and others, domestic violence is abuse against an intimate partner used to gain power and control. Through the systemic use of these

2. Herman, Trauma and Recovery, 74

types of behaviors, perpetrators have controlled their intimate partners throughout history. But our increased societal focus on property ownership and the privatization of the household over the last two-thousand years has exacerbated this practice.[3]

In the modern-day context of the United States, the problems of domestic violence and its deleterious effects on individuals and communities have seemingly become common sense. The civil-rights movement of the 1960s grounds the public awareness and engagement around domestic violence. Before the 1970s, the fields of trauma research and the larger field of psychology, were mostly focused on men's experiences of trauma, specifically war. But beginning in the 70s, the women's movement brought experiences of gender-based violence and oppression into the spotlight. The reality was that the experiences of abuse that women face in their everyday civilian lives were more common than traumas experienced by soldiers.[4] The women's movement allowed women to break the silence of their private, domestic worlds, leading to the public awareness around issues of domestic violence we experience currently in the United States. But history does not guarantee that this societal awareness and progress on women's rights to health and happiness will remain to be our reality. Awareness, education, and systemic change are crucial for us to maintain and expand women's equality.

Description and Statistics

"When the victim is already devalued (a woman, a child), she may find that the most traumatic event of her life takes place outside the realm of socially validated reality. Her experience becomes unspeakable."

JUDITH HERMAN[5]

Despite the surge in knowledge and response that defines our current context, domestic violence remains a pervasive problem for many people around the world. Looking specifically at the experience of heterosexual women in the United States, *The National Intimate Partner and Sexual Violence Survey* of 2010 found that close to one in three women (30.3 percent) had been physically abused by a partner in their lifetime. The same survey the following year found that 4 percent of women had experienced

3. Dobash and Dobash, *Violence against Wives.*
4. Herman, *Trauma and Recovery*, 28.
5. Herman, *Trauma and Recovery*, 8.

some form of physical violence just within the past year. When the survey questions expanded beyond physical violence to include psychological aggression, the survey found that almost half of women (48.4 percent) in the United States experienced abuse during their lifetimes.[6] Despite our movements towards gender parity in the public conversation, the home and women private lives remain spaces of inequality.

The nature of intimate partner violence is such that anyone can be a survivor; it affects people across gender, age, race, nationality, and sexual orientation. That being said, these identity markers do shape people's experiences of abuse, the barriers they may face, and the resources available to them. For example, while both men and women can be survivors of domestic violence, according to the United States Department of Justice's Bureau of Justice Statistics, the majority of victims (4 in 5) are females. The majority of perpetrators of violence, on the other hand, are male (90 percent).[7] Throughout this book, I purposefully use female gendered pronouns as the default for survivors to reflect this gendered reality. I do not intend to erase male-survivors, who also face barriers to justice and equality, but rather I hope to strategically highlight the gendered history and reality of abuse.

Also, while women of all ages experience domestic violence, almost half (47.1 percent) of survivors have their first experience of intimate partner violence between the ages of 18 and 24.[8] This equates to one in six women under the age of 24 having experienced violence at the hands of their partner. While age does not cause or preclude someone from intimate partner violence, perpetrators seem to take advantage of the young adult years of identity formation and growing independence from one's family of origin.

Similarly, women of all races experience domestic violence and while race alone is not a factor in who experiences abuse, it does act as a factor in how survivors experience the abuse and obtain help. In the United States, "an estimated 51.7 percent of American Indian/Alaska Native women, 51.3 percent of multiracial women, 41.2 percent of non-Hispanic black women, 30.5 percent of non-Hispanic white women, 29.7 percent of Hispanic women, and 15.3 percent of Asian or Pacific Islander

6. Black, *The National Intimate Partner*, 55. This number stays the same for men as well, with almost half of men in the United States experiencing psychological aggression at the hand of an intimate partner in their lifetime.

7. Kimmel, "'Gender Symmetry' in Domestic Violence."

8. Black, *The National Intimate Partner*, 59.

women experienced physical violence by an intimate partner during their lifetimes."[9] Researchers speculate that the higher rates of violence for multiracial and American Indian/Alaska Native are connected to higher rates of poverty, social and geographic isolation, and alcohol use by the perpetrator.[10] Scholars have also pointed out that in the United States, resources for domestic violence survivors who are also women of color are underdeveloped and underfunded.[11]

Domestic violence is a reality that also stretches across all sexual orientations. Research on intimate partner violence within the LGBT community has lagged behind research on heterosexual partners. Generalizing about LGBT domestic violence is also problematic because studies that focus on these communities suffer from smaller sampling and variations in defining both "LGBT relationships" and "intimate partner violence." Overall, lesbian women experience statistically similar amounts of abuse as their straight counterparts. Gay men, on the other hand, experience higher rates of abuse in intimate relationships than heterosexual men. Research focused on bisexual women and men is even rarer, but the studies that are available seem to suggest bisexual women and men are at greater risk for abuse. Research studies on transgender persons and intimate partner violence are largely absent, but some qualitative data exists to suggest transgender persons experience abuse at similar to higher rates to heteronormative persons.[12]

Survivors of domestic violence can suffer from a number of physical and mental side effects, resulting from the traumatic nature of the experience. In general, trauma is understood as an event or events in which a person encounters death, but survives. This can include a threat to their life or bodily integrity. This can also include experiencing it directly or witnessing the event of someone else. The psychological effects of traumatic events, such as domestic violence, stem from the difficulty

9. Breiding, "Prevalence and Characteristics," 11.

10. Bachman et al., *Violence against American Indian and Alaska Native Women.*

11. Adams, *Woman-Battering*, 32. Womanist scholars are correct in pointing to the layering of discrimination experienced by women of color. Womanist scholar Toinnette M Eugene argues that for Black women the social services in our society (police, social workers, etc.) have already failed them so many times that these communities of women have become isolated, leading to the increase of misinformation about issues such as domestic violence and abuse. She calls the black community to action, specifically to protect and refrain from hurting each other, arguing that the community experiences enough violence from the outside world. Eugene, "'Swing Low, Sweet Chariot!,'" 187.

12. See Walters and Lippy, "Intimate Partner Violence in LGBT Communities."

survivors face in narrating their experience. While other parts of the brain, such as the limbic system, are hyper-active, making us aware of our surroundings, our bodies in space, sights, smells, and sounds, the frontal cortex of the brain, which is responsible for language processing, functions very little during a traumatic experience.[13] These body processes, which dampen the logic centers of the brain, results in traumatic memories rarely taking on narrative form.[14] As a result of these unique biological trauma responses, the brain stores traumatic memory differently than other types of memories, often resulting in memories that are difficult for people to process verbally and can cause mental health crises for survivors.

Survivors of domestic violence report a higher prevalence of physical health issues as well, such as "asthma, irritable bowel syndrome, diabetes, frequent headaches, chronic pain, difficulty sleeping, and activity limitations."[15] Overall, survivors of violence are three times more likely to rate their physical or mental health as poor in comparison to those who have not experienced domestic violence.[16] Domestic violence costs our society billions of dollars every year in healthcare costs and lost productivity. While difficult to pinpoint, the CDC estimates that in one year (2003) domestic violence cost the United States 8.3 billion dollars,[17] showing us that this issue is not only prevalent, but also extremely costly.

The Road to Recovery

"The women who recover most successfully are those who discover some meaning in their experience that transcends the limits of personal tragedy."

JUDITH HERMAN[18]

In connecting domestic violence with the larger psychological field of trauma research, Judith Herman's groundbreaking work in *Trauma and*

13. See van der Kolk, *The Body Keeps Score*.

14. See Levine, *In an Unspoken Voice*. Another physiologist, Peter Levine, talks about this moment and space the body inhabits in trauma as a unique state that the body should embrace rather than fight against. Levine argues that it is when we fight against the natural processes of the body dealing with trauma that the disconnection between our brain and body occurs and creates post-traumatic stress symptoms.

15. Black, *The National Intimate Partner*, 72.

16. Black, *The National Intimate Partner*, 72.

17. Max et al., "The Economic Toll of Intimate Partner Violence."

18. Herman, *Trauma and Recovery*, 73.

Recovery outlines three stages for recovery that reflect the healing journeys of trauma survivors of all types. These stages are not literal steps that are followed one after the other until survivors are done healing. Rather, survivors gradually shift from "unpredictable danger to reliable safety" along their healing process.[19] The first stage is to establish safety. Survivors of trauma cannot begin to move towards stability until they have established their physical and emotional safety. This is especially true for domestic violence survivors, who often remain intimately connected to their source of trauma.

The second stage is the need for remembrance and mourning. Survivors need to have time to remember, talk about, and process their experience, as well as grieve their losses. In situations of domestic violence, losses could include the relationship or their life before the abuse and survivors need time to mourn and acknowledge these losses. The traumatic nature of domestic violence makes it so that the healing responses and needs of survivors will be unique to other forms of processing suffering or pain.

Finally, survivors must reconnect with ordinary life. Survivors need to be able to return to a semblance of normalcy for them. Herman also acknowledges that, while not necessary for recovery, women who discover "meaning in their experience that transcends the limits of personal tragedy" recover more successfully than those who do not. For example, those survivors who became active in the anti-rape movement actually recovered more successfully.[20] This is true for domestic violence survivors as well. Working in the community to raise awareness and provide resources for others who have experienced domestic violence can be an important part of someone's healing journey.

Domestic violence disconnects survivors from the world and others, but at the same time, their connection to the world and others is key to their healing process. The stages of recovery above all require establishing safe and trustworthy relationships of support. The nature of trauma and survivors' disconnection from their world means that social and community support is crucial to establish safety, help restore the survivor's identity, and help mourn the loss experienced. After their identity is put into jeopardy by a traumatic event, survivors are left to rebuild their identities in similar ways to when they were younger and first developing their sense of self. As young children, our families and the community that

19. Herman, *Trauma and Recovery*, 155.

20. Herman, *Trauma and Recovery*, 73.

supports our growth shape our identity. Unfortunately, survivors must forge a new identity that includes their experiences of trauma. As with all life experiences, our identities are left changed. Similarly, these experiences of trauma force survivors to change as well.[21] The communal aspects of identity formation are why trauma recovery must include empowering relationships and cannot happen without those relationships in place.

Unfortunately, for domestic violence survivors their relationships have been part of their trauma. When a relationship is abusive, the complexity and influence of close relationships become problematic. Many survivors find support groups to be an important and integral part of their healing process, creating a safe space completely disconnected from the abusive relationship. Relationships between survivors and their therapist, close friends, or family, play important roles in survivors' healing, but the larger community has an important role to play as well. Specifically, the community must help establish these public spaces that recognize the trauma of domestic violence and provide restitution for survivors.

The vast number of women and men affected, its non-discriminating nature, and its long-standing history in our society, all make domestic violence a difficult and complex problem to undertake. The multifaceted and layered causes of violence are also difficult to sort through. The systems of oppression that allow domestic violence to continue in these pandemic proportions are deeply rooted in our cultures. In the United States today, we consider the physically violent actions of a perpetrator of abuse to be illegal. But throughout the majority of history, and still in many parts of the world, society has accepted these types of behaviors and continues to consider them normal for the patriarch of a family.

Societal Roots of Domestic Violence

"Women did not have a name for the tyranny of private life. It was difficult to recognize that a well-established democracy in the public sphere could coexist with conditions of primitive autocracy or advanced dictatorship in the home."

JUDITH HERMAN[22]

As we have discussed, domestic violence is not an anomaly to our current context, but rather connected to our society's historical assumptions

21. Herman, *Trauma and Recovery*, 93.
22. Herman, Trauma and Recovery, 28

about gender and power. In fact, today abuse towards an intimate partner does not necessarily signify that a perpetrator suffers from a behavioral or mental disorder. Abusers often purposefully choose these types of behaviors as strategic and effective tactics to control a relationship. The general consensus of activists and researchers in the field of domestic violence is that the prevalence of these abusive behaviors is not a signal that men are inherently more violent, but rather that our society has shaped traditional masculinity to be synonymous with power and control. We can see this globally, but societies that stress patriarchal dominance are at particular risk. For example, when comparing university students of different cultural backgrounds, students whose cultural norms reinforced male dominance and the use of violence were significantly more likely to use physical and psychological abusive behaviors against dating partners.[23]

In the United States, the legacy of the Roman Empire shapes our current understandings of the individual, property ownership, and the household.[24] Through the expanse of Rome and the adoption of this patriarchal, male-ruled structure by early Christians, the Roman household became the functioning norm for much of western history. By sanctifying the home, western culture treated the household as a private matter and pushed it outside the public eye. Over time, the medieval household solidified property ownership and the transaction of property through male members of families, resulting in husbands acquiring their wife's land and property directly from her father. In addition, women experienced a further loss of agency during this time period through the separation of love and marriage, courtly romance, and codes of chivalry, that glorified and commodified them as property. Continuing forward, during the industrial age and the rise of capitalism, the devaluation of domestic work made women even more economically dependent on their husbands. Alongside the increasing privatization of property and the household, the idea and structures of individualism also grew, resulting in a double-bind that persists today for women, who society considers unwomanly when they exercise their agency and incompetent or childlike when they don't.[25] Women and men, caught in this double bind, find it impossible to satisfy cultural expectations. Each of these technological and social developments eroded the agency of women and other minorities in society

23. Ozaki and Otis. "Gender Equality."

24. See Dobash and Dobash, *Violence against Wives*, 34–50.

25. Young-Eisendrath and Wehr, "The Fallacy of Individualism," 120–23.

resulting in them facing the violent consequences of breaking societal norms, such as battering, rape, or trafficking.

These forces shape perpetrators of abuse as well, and to say a perpetrator is individually accountable alone, allows society to scapegoat one person and ignore the larger problem. In reality, we are all culpable as part of a society that shapes and allows domestic violence. No one is innocent when domestic violence is understood as a systemic problem. When we reject the separation of "victims," "perpetrators," and the larger society, we reframe the issue of domestic violence as a systemic and societal problem, extending outside the private sphere of personal relationships.[26] Today, the societal move to frame perpetrators as monstrous anomalies ignores the larger cultural forces that shape toxic masculinity and create systems of exploitation and oppression. Perpetrators need to be held accountable, but we must also address the inherent gender inequities of our society, which result in a climate where domestic violence and abuse can flourish.

Domestic Violence and Religion: An Immeasurable Relationship

"If there is any hope of stopping physical and sexual abuse, leaders of the church need to join social workers, police, lawyers, psychologist, and judges in educating the public and developing systems of accountability."

MARIE M. FORTUNE AND JAMES POLING[27]

Over the last forty years, researchers have brought the tools of statistical analysis to the issue of domestic violence hoping its connection to religion would become clear. Unfortunately, this was not necessarily the case. While there is no singular clear statistical correlation between religion and domestic violence, the relationship remains complex and an important reality for any theologian or practitioner with which to wrestle. First, many sociologists and psychologists are interested in the possibility that religious beliefs might help or harm survivors of abuse. Do religious beliefs legitimize or forbid abuse against women? Practitioners and theologians have investigated the role of scripture in the perpetration of abuse as well, showing that scripture defies singular interpretations.

26. Enns, *The Violence of Victimhood*, 11.

27. Fortune and Poling, "Calling to Accountability," 453.

Many sociologists and pastoral care researchers are most concerned with whether religion provides positive or negative resources in healing from abuse. Additionally, we must consider the effects of a traumatic experience like domestic violence on an individual's belief system. All of these different questions about the connection between religion and domestic violence defy a singular answer. But, again, this remains a fruitful exploration for the church, revealing the necessary complexity in any theological response to domestic violence.

Religion:
A Risk or Protective Factor

Psychological and sociological research, conducted to explore the relationship between religion and domestic violence, shows that overall religiosity has little to no effect on whether someone experiences or perpetuates abuse. Religiosity neither protects families from abuse nor increases the likelihood of abuse. In one study, conducted with a cross section of Canadian adults, who were married or cohabitating, it was shown that religious persuasion had little to no effect on spousal abuse. The level of religious belief and practice did not influence an abuser's choice to abuse or not to abuse their partner. The only significant findings in this study were that more conservative Christian women were slightly more likely to abuse their husbands than other women and women who were more successful than their spouses were at higher risk to experience abuse.[28] Another study found that while partners who have different religious traditions are not more at risk than partners who share religious traditions, men who are more conservative in their religious values than their partners perpetrate domestic violence at higher rates.[29] But at the same time, religious attendance is inversely linked to domestic violence.[30] Specifically, men and women who attend worship once a week and women who attend once a month are less likely to perpetrate violence.[31] We cannot assume causation from these statistics. It is unknown whether weekly attendance makes someone less likely to abuse, or if people who

---

28. Brinkerhoof et al., "Religious Involvement and Spousal Violence."

29. Ellison et al., "Are There Religious Variations in Domestic Violence?"

30. Ellison et al., "Are There Religious Variations in Domestic Violence?"

31. Ellison and Anderson, "Religious Involvement and Domestic Violence."

are less likely to abuse attend religious services more often than abusers. Or there may be a third correlated factor that we are not considering.

What is significant about these findings is that they show anyone can experience domestic violence, irrespective of religious tradition. Sociologist Nancy Nason-Clark argues that while religious families experience abuse at the same rates as non-religious families, religious women are more vulnerable when abused.[32] Because of the pressure many religious traditions put on the sanctity of the traditional family, religious women may feel guilty leaving their marriages or that the situation is somehow their fault, and are, in general, less likely to leave. A different study found that survivor's religious beliefs influenced the cycle of leaving and returning to an abusive relationship. M. N. Burnett discusses the need for pastoral language that is sensitive to survivors of domestic violence and understands that women who are experiencing abuse may believe they should stay in their violent situation in order to honor their marriage vows. Burnett argues that religious authorities should actively work with victims of abuse, making sure to free them from their sense of marital obligation to their abuser.[33] This poses a particular challenge in churches with solely male leadership, making it even more crucial that the full church community denounces domestic violence. Religious institutions cannot ignore the issue of domestic violence, and when domestic violence affects one in three of the women in their communities, religious leaders and communities must address this issue.

The Effects of Scripture

"The only way that the Bible can be regarded as straightforward and simple is if no one bothers to read it."

JENNIFER KNUST[34]

A similarly opaque connection lies between domestic violence and scriptural readings. The texts we find within the Hebrew Bible and the New Testament are far from univocal when it comes to the use of violence. These texts are similarly troublesome for those seeking guidance within a marriage. Throughout the majority of Christian history abusers, in the

32. Nason-Clark, "When Terror Strikes at Home," 304.

33. Burnett, "Suffering and Sanctification."

34. Knust, *Unprotected Texts*, 10.

role of husbands and father, have used the Hebrew and Christian texts to keep their patriarchal hold on their families. They point to texts such as the Pauline letter to the Ephesians as proof that God has given them power over their families. The passage, attributed to Paul, reads "Wives, be subject to your husbands as you are to the Lord. For the husband is the head of the wife just as Christ is the head of the church, the body of which he is the Savior. Just as the church is subject to Christ, so also wives ought to be, in everything, to their husbands." This passage, while one of the most troubling for progressive Christians, is commonly referred to by abusers in order to justify abusive behavior.[35]

Abuse and rape of women appear throughout the biblical texts and are often for the benefit or punishment of the male protagonists. These stories are not just outdated, harmless aspects of the tradition. These passages echo the reality many women continue to face today, but in uncritical and dangerous ways.[36] They function in our imaginations, churches, and families in ways that cannot be fully calculated. In an attempt to begin to show the societal effects of these violent texts, Brad J. Bushman and colleagues found in a psychological study that scriptural texts in which God sanctioned violence increased aggression in subjects, especially if they identified as "believers" of the text.[37] When read as uncritical moral guidelines, scripture is extremely harmful, promoting oppressive structures such as slavery, abuse, and victim blaming.

While scripture that promotes violence or inequality negatively influences our lives, scripture that liberates can have positive effects. More and more, scholars and practitioners have turned to scripture to seek messages of liberation and human worth. Feminist biblical scholars, such as Elisabeth Schüssler Fiorenza, have worked to reclaim these dangerous texts for women. Schüssler Fiorenza specifically argues that patriarchal and hierarchical texts break with original, egalitarian practices of the Christian church. These passages, such as Ephesians 5:22, are less about the community of Jesus, his followers, and early Christians and more about later Christian communities cloaking themselves in the Greco-Roman household codes as a response to Roman hostility towards Christians.[38]

35. See Loue, "Family Violence and Abuse."

36. See Cooper-White, *The Cry of Tamar.*

37. Bushman et al., "When God Sanctions Killing."

38. See Schüssler Fiorenza, *In Memory of Her*; and Starkey "The Roman Catholic Church and Violence against Women."

The oppressed of history have always been able to find the liberative aspects of scripture and this holds true for women as well. In one study, Shondrah Tarrezz Nash looked at the scriptural interpretations of women who experienced abuse. She hoped to see if and how their experience of abuse affected their reading of scripture, as well as, how the reading may affect the narrating of their abuse experience. Nash found that the hermeneutical theory, which argues "despite the time of its origin, once a text is recorded, its meaning is independent of the author's intent and the circumstances that produced it," was upheld and that the women subverted more traditionally oppressive texts about submission in light of their experience of abuse.[39] Nash found it was natural for women to reflect on their own experiences of abuse and oppression while reading and interpreting the scripture in ways that subverted, rather than reinforced, the traditionally patriarchal interpretation of text.

Domestic Violence's Effects on Religious Beliefs

"Wounded soldiers and raped women cry for their mothers, or for God. When this cry is not answered, the sense of basic trust is shattered. Traumatized people feel utterly abandoned, utterly alone, cast out of the human and divine systems of care and protection that sustain life."

JUDITH HERMAN[40]

Above, we looked at how religious beliefs and practices affect rates of domestic violence, but it is also important to consider the effects of this relationship in the opposite direction. Does the experience of domestic violence shape survivors' religious lives more negatively or positively? Again, this question does not have a clear answer. Most studies and anecdotal reports suggest that survivors embrace their religious lives more fully in the wake of domestic violence, pulling on their faith and the religious community for support in their healing journey. The vast majority of survivors cite their spirituality or God as a source of comfort after an experience of violence.[41] But this does not address the underlying

39. Nash, "Changing of the Gods," 199.

40. Herman, *Trauma and Recovery*, 52.

41. Gillum, Sullivan, and Bybee, "The Importance of Spirituality in the Lives of Domestic Violence Survivors," 240.

question of whether domestic violence reshapes the way survivors think theologically.

While there is little sociological and psychological research on the theological effects of domestic violence on religious beliefs, the effect of trauma, more generally, on religious belief has been studied. One study conducted by Wendy S. Overcash and colleagues compared the religious beliefs of a group of trauma survivors with a control group of non-trauma survivors. The researchers wondered how trauma affected religious beliefs, hypothesizing that trauma would bring religious beliefs into question, resulting in less faith in the trauma group as compared to the control group. The researchers found that experiences of trauma were correlated with greater psychological distress, but there was no significant difference in the trauma groups' satisfaction with life. At the center of the study was the finding that trauma did not affect their religious beliefs— rather the religious beliefs provided a narrative frame for understanding the traumatic experience. Also, contrary to common thought, the core metaphysical belief (how God works in the world) was left completely unchanged.[42] Studies such as this would suggest personal belief systems more often remain steadfast in the wake of domestic violence and provide a narrative frame for survivors' traumatic experiences. Religion is an important part of the lives and decision-making processes for many people. When people experience a crisis, they often turn towards their religious beliefs, practices, and communities for support and strength, rather than turning away or questioning them. This seems to be true for survivors of domestic violence as well, considering the majority of survivors seek help from their religious communities.[43] But further research is needed to more fully understand the effects of domestic violence on the theological frameworks of survivors.

Religion as a Resource for Recovery

While many aspects of the relationship between domestic violence and organized religion are circuitous, survivors of domestic violence by and large report that their personal faith and spirituality are positive resources for their recovery. One psychological study found that 97 percent of

42. Overcash et al., "Coping with Crises."

43. See Nason-Clark, *The Battered Wife*, 41; and Horton et al., "Women Who Ended Abuse."

survivors of violence saw their personal faith as a source of strength and almost all the women cited that their religious beliefs were part of their healing journey. On top of that, their religious involvement was a predictor of increased psychological well-being and decreased depression.[44] Professor of Nursing, Janice Humphreys, found a similar relationship between faith and mental health of domestic violence survivors. In her study of 50 women over 7 months at a domestic violence shelter, spirituality was correlated to less distress and depression. She argued that spirituality may provide internal resources for calming the mind, distancing distressing feelings, and connecting oneself to a higher power.[45] While in an abusive relationship, victims often live their daily lives in a heightened state of stress, focusing on survival over self-actualization. This results in a restricted space for psychological or spiritual growth, because safety becomes the priority. But once survivors leave their restrictive relationships, they are able to develop their spirituality in ways that assist in healing and connecting back to themselves, others, life, and God.

Unfortunately, the effects of more organized forms of religious response on survivors' recovery is more varied. Studies show that many survivors of domestic violence turn to religious communities, with over half of women reporting that they sought help from a religious authority.[46] But, most survivors who reach out to religious authorities leave dissatisfied with the experience, citing issues such as, being given bad advice (i.e. wear him out with sex), that the clergy member had little to no idea how to respond, or even being accused by the clergy member of lying.[47] In addition, research shows that pastors tend to have a skewed view of the reality of domestic violence. Many clergy recognize that couples experience abuse, but often underestimate its effect on their community. The average pastor believes that 28 percent of married couples experience

44. Gillum et al., "The Importance of Spirituality in the Lives of Domestic Violence Survivors," 240.

45. Humphreys, "Spirituality and Distress in Sheltered Battered Women." See also, Horton et al., "Women Who Ended Abuse/" Horton et al. found that 24 percent of participants found faith to be a comfort, providing them strength and even in about 5 percent of cases keeping them from suicide. But on the other side of the coin, 20 percent of participants cited their religion as the reason they stayed in the abusive relationship.

46. See Nason-Clark, The Battered Wife, 41. And Horton, Wilkins, and Wright, "Women Who Ended Abuse."

47. Horton, Wilkins, and Wright, "Women Who Ended Abuse." See also Bowker, "Religious Victim and Their Religious Leaders," 232.

abuse (close to the 30 percent reality), but also believes that only 18 percent of their congregation experiences abuse.[48] For many survivors, education on the pervasiveness of domestic violence can be a turning point in their ability to see their own relationship as unhealthy. Not only are pastors often approached by survivors, but they address their communities weekly and can use their place of privilege to educate their congregation, condemn violence, and challenge patriarchal systems.[49]

Sociologist of Religion, Nancy Nason-Clark connects these problematic responses and lack of knowledge on behalf of clergy to the church's history of functioning as a part of the patriarchal power structure in society, acting as a place where perpetrators can commit violence and abuse. In her book, *The Battered Wife: How Christians Confront Family Violence,* Nason-Clark argues that on top of cultural inequality, the privatization of the household has worked to keep women within the private sphere, isolating them from help or support with domestic violence.[50] This has continued to be true and worsen as nuclear families become more and more isolated. Clergy education and awareness on these issues can help to mitigate the negative responses survivors receive and increase the likelihood of a positive experience. Many churches have predominantly responded through clergy and pastoral training. Unfortunately, clergy often self-select into these trainings, meaning that training only reaches those who are already somewhat aware of the issue of abuse. These clergy-focused programs also do not address the possibilities of larger community response.

Pastors not only have an obligation to the survivors of violence in their communities, but also to perpetrators of violence. Churches have the difficult job of providing safe space for women and children, while also understanding that perpetrators are also present in their communities.

---

48. Nason-Clark, *The Battered Wife,* 59.

49. See Nason-Clark, *The Battered Wife,* 148–53.

50. See Nason-Clark, *The Battered Wife.* Nason-Clark cites movements such as "promise keepers," a men's ministry focused on traditional male roles and masculinity, as strengthening the male dominant model of the family, which remains prevalent for many throughout the United States and Canada. Even more dangerous are programs such as Dr. James Dobson's "Focus on the Family," which touts that tough love alone can work to create a healthy marriage, even if these tactics are only practiced by one side of the partnership. The danger in this type of language and programming is that in an abusive relationship the full onus of change is placed on the victim, who has, by the definition of domestic violence, less control and power in the relationship than their partner.

Keeping in mind many perpetrators may also be or have been victims, clergy have a unique role to play in providing pastoral care *and* accountability to abusers. Statistics show that pastors and other religious leaders have the power to hold abusers accountable on par with judicial institutions. Perpetrators are more likely to complete domestic violence treatment programs if they are referred by clergy than a judge. Completion rates are highest when both the religious and judicial systems are involved.[51] Accountability is one of the only ways perpetrators can change their behavior, and religious communities can't provide accountability unless they are aware and informed on the nature of domestic violence. Perpetrators are one piece of the domestic violence issue, one that society often ignores, denies, or ostracizes. Avoiding the problems that come with the presence of a perpetrator in a church community, by either pushing them out of the community or ignoring them, only continues the cycle of violence. That person will possibly continue on to a new community and find new partners to control and abuse. Far from blaming the victim for the future violence of a perpetrator, the community is held responsible as a whole. Only in sharing the responsibility can we actually break the cycle of violence.[52]

On top of pastoral care for survivors and perpetrators, religious communities can work closely with nonprofits to alleviate the problems of domestic violence. Partnerships between religious and secular services are extremely important for both sides, helping to bridge the gaps in each other's networks and services. Secular services can provide temporary shelter, legal services, and crisis counseling, while churches provide a consistent community, providing support in more personal ways, as well as addressing questions of faith and providing spiritual practices of healing.[53] Many religiously conservative women don't seek out secular services because they fear secular counselors or advocates will not take their faith seriously.[54] But, by working together, everyone's needs can be met, especially through the social networks provided by religious communities.

Other women in a religious community become an important resource for those isolated by abuse. Nason-Clark found that over half of

51. Nason-Clark, "When Terror Strikes at Home," 305.

52. See Fortune and Poling, "Calling to Accountability."

53. See Gillum et al., "The Importance of Spirituality in the Lives of Domestic Violence Survivors," 248.

54. Nason-Clark, *The Battered Wife*, 140.

the women in her study had provided some kind of support, with 91.9 percent of those women providing at least a listening ear.[55] The role of religious community support is especially true for women of color.[56] Integrated into the support provided by others in the religious community are the religious and spiritual beliefs and practices that help to provide healing for many survivors of domestic violence. The research suggests that spiritual and religious practices, beliefs, and communities have the potential to support women healing from domestic violence. While clergy training and response has varied in the past decades, the larger religious community—especially other women—has continued to provide a network of support, helping survivors to reconnect and access the resources they need.

Theological Investigations and Response: Roots of Engagement

"By refusing to endure evil and by seeking to transform suffering, we are about God's work of making justice and healing brokenness."

MARIE M. FORTUNE[57]

The work of feminist theologians in the 1980s and 1990s, who brought to light the inherent gender biases found in the Christian religious tradition and our theological conversations, shaped much of the initial theological conversation and response around domestic violence. Feminist theologians, such as Rosemary Radford Ruether, narrated the subordination of women throughout history, beginning with early pre-Christian thinkers such as Aristotle, who subordinated women by arguing females were literally "misbegotten males." These philosophers believed women were essentially born with the birth defect of being female. Early Christian thinkers, like Augustine and Aquinas, utilized these philosophies of gender to argue that God did not create females in God's image, like their male counterparts, and therefore females could not serve in the priesthood

---

55. Nason-Clark, *The Battered Wife*, 117.

56. See Watlington and Murphy, "The Roles of Religion and Spirituality."

57. Fortune, "The Transformation of Suffering," 91.

because they did not represent Christ by their nature.[58] Arguments for the inferiority of women and their essential difference from their male counterparts have led to a long history of churches and church authorities supporting a hierarchical structure to the Christian family. In addition, churches have historically supported the husband's right to chastise his wife based on the concern with property ownership. If church authorities were to argue for the rights of women in marriage, governments might challenge church property ownership.[59] Unfortunately, theology has historically been constructed around the male experience and the concerns of women have continued to fall outside the concerns of churches.

Another compounding variable in churches' responses to domestic violence is the long-established tradition of anti-sexuality and the condemnation of the body. For example, during the Reformation, Luther believed that males should have power over females in order to carry out their punishment for the fall and original sin. The church has used all of this to justify centuries of mistreating women, which seemed to reach a peak of violence during the centuries of the late Middle Ages to the end of the seventeenth century, which included the practice of "witch hunting." Church and societal leaders targeted females, who were considered fair game for punishment because they were believed to be prone to demonic possession. When society was faced with a perceived threat against the immortal souls of their women, there wasn't much they wouldn't do to "save them," including burning, drowning, and torturing them.[60]

Early feminist theologians of the 1980s had uncovered a disturbing reality, narrating a history of abuse at the center of the Christian tradition. In conversation with these theologians, pastoral theologians were beginning to narrate the specific crisis of domestic violence within church communities. In her book, *Battered Women: From a Theology of Suffering to an Ethic of Empowerment*, Joy Bussert describes the silence kept by churches and clergy (either out of pride or denial) about the issue of domestic violence up through the 1980s. Her book was one that helped to break that silence, and in 1986 paved the way for theologians and others to step into dialogue with the Church about domestic violence. While this early book helped to bring domestic violence to the fore for clergy and laypeople, it was not without its problems: such as psychologizing

58. See Radford Ruether, "The Western Religious Tradition," 32–33.

59. Bohn, "Dominion to Rule," 106–9. This also plays into the slow response many Christian churches had to slavery.

60. Radford Ruether, "The Western Religious Tradition," 33–37.

abusers' behaviors and simplifying abuse without connecting it to the larger systemic problems of patriarchy. By 1988, a few years later, Anne L. Horton and Judith A. Williamson made an argument, similar to Bussert, that the Church as an institution must change and more fully address the issue of domestic violence.[61]

The following decade, feminist theologians wrestled with the deep theological implications of this history of abuse within the Christian tradition. With the books and scholars above opening up the conversation between domestic violence and theology in the late 1980s, the 1990s saw a number of theological engagements by feminist theologians on the topic of domestic violence and discerning how to proceed. Feminist theologians were giving survivors of domestic violence a theological voice and a seat at the table, challenging a number of theological assumptions, most prominently of which were questions of suffering, evil, and forgiveness.

Joanne Carlson Brown and Carole R Bohn's 1989 edited volume, *Christianity, Patriarchy, and Abuse: A Feminist Critique,* investigated a number of theological topics that clashed with the lived experiences of domestic violence and sexual abuse survivors. In one chapter of this volume, Marie Fortune searches for the meaning and purpose of suffering. As the 1977 founder of the Faith Trust Institute, which works to end domestic violence from an interfaith position, Fortune has a long history of working on the issue of domestic violence. She uses her decades of experience to probe questions about the meaning of suffering and evil in light of domestic violence. Theodicy, the theological problem of evil, traditionally seeks a way of making sense of suffering in a world where God is all-powerful and all good. For survivors of violence, their experiences of suffering and violence challenges the idea that God is both omnipotent and good. Fortune acknowledges that for many survivors of violence the most logical thing to do is to blame themselves or God. Survivors often find that blaming themselves helps to bring some semblance of control back into their lives. But Fortune points to a third party: the perpetrator.[62] When trying to understand evil in light of domestic violence, we must consider the human sinfulness of the perpetrator.

Another theological issue covered in Fortune's chapter is the "problem of endurance" and theologies that forget to seek transformation. The "problem of endurance" is the belief that something is gained in

---

61. Horton and Williamson, *Abuse and Religion,* 10.

62. See Fortune, "The Transformation of Suffering," 140–42

enduring suffering; we get stuck looking for the greater good and trying to narrate our experience of evil in this type language. Fortune argues that because there is *"no greater good* for anyone" in the experience of domestic violence or sexual abuse there is nothing gained by enduring it. Rather, Fortune turns to the experience of transformation, using the example of Jesus' resurrection after the crucifixion. The resurrection in no way justifies the suffering on the cross, Fortune argues, but we should understand the reality that suffering and evil exist and work to help each other transform through hope and empowerment. Fortune concludes that "By refusing to endure evil and by seeking to transform suffering, we are about God's work of making justice and healing brokenness."[63]

Feminist theologians and scholars have also critiqued theologies that focus on forgiveness. In another theological piece, Fortune notes that we often tie forgiveness to hopes of closure and the end of a painful experience, but stresses that it should be a *last* step in the healing process. Fortune argues that justice, which works to protect the vulnerable by breaking the silence and telling the truth, is a precondition to forgiveness. Unfortunately for many, justice is never achieved. Offenders must be held accountable before they can be forgiven. Also, we often conflate forgiveness and forgetting in our theologies of forgiveness. Fortune believes forgiveness is about no longer allowing the memory of the abuse to continue to abuse and not about forgetting the abuse. Fortune calls forgetting the abuse, or forgiving too soon, cheap forgiveness and argues that this is unhelpful and dangerous for survivors.[64] Feminist theologians have long grappled with theologies of forgiveness. What if justice is never achieved? Should the failure of the system continue to punish survivors, keeping them tied to the memory of abuse until society can serve them justice? While theologians continue to construct and deconstruct theologies of forgiveness, Fortune's contribution to the conversation is important because it brings "cheap forgiveness" into questions and challenges the pressure survivors often face within church communities to forgive.

Church Response: An Ecumenical Summary

Feminist theologians also contributed greatly to the development and continued education around the pastoral response to domestic violence.

63. See Fortune, "The Transformation of Suffering," 145–47.
64. See Fortune, "Forgiveness: The Last Step," 201–6.

Over the past several decades, church communities have continued to grow and strengthen their responses to domestic violence through a number of ways; and the feminist theological conversation has helped give theological language to this issue for church communities. The church community and persons of authority, such as pastors, provide unique resources that can help survivors process their experience, provide practical assistance, and reflect theologically. They can also keep survivors safe by understanding the dangers and pitfalls of traditional pastoral care, such as couples counseling, in situations of abuse and the importance of making other types of referrals. Ideally, pastors play a crucial role in denouncing abusive behavior and holding abusers in their community accountable. At their best, churches play a crucial healing and liberative role in the lives of survivors of abuse. The Christian church's responses to domestic violence is far from monolithic. Each Christian community has a unique history and approach to issues of violence against women, each with their own strengths and weaknesses in their responses to domestic violence.

The Catholic Church

While the Catholic church has a rich tradition of working for social justice, its response to domestic violence has been marred by the church's early rejection of modernity, including social sciences like psychology and sociology. It wasn't until 1967, through Vatican II, that the church opened itself up to the wisdom of the social sciences and global civil rights concerns. The changes implemented by Vatican II opened up a number of roles for women in the church, giving women and their concerns more presence in the public church. One significant Vatican II document that helped to broaden women's roles in the church was the Pastoral Constitution on the Church in the Modern World, *Gaudium et spes*. This document also highlights the importance and role of the spousal partnership. But like the vast majority of church documents, which address issues of marriage, *Gaudium et spes* neglects to address issues of domestic violence and abuse in the household.

One document put forth by the United States Conference of Catholic Bishops (USCCB), entitled "When I Call for Help," addresses this issue directly and attempts to advise survivors, abusers, pastors, and the larger society in responding to domestic violence. The bishops originally wrote the document in 1992, but they have updated it most recently in

2002. The most significant aspect of this documents is that the bishops are unequivocal in their rejection of violence against women and name it a sin, as well as a crime. This document also makes it clear that scholars, clergy, and laity should never use the Bible in a way that supports abusive behavior in any form, rather "a correct reading of Scripture leads people to an understanding of the equal dignity of men and women and to relationships based on mutuality and love."[65]

In addition to these statements against domestic violence, there are several aspects of the Catholic worldview that lend themselves to positively responding to violence and suffering. The sacramental worldview, which sees the presence of God in creation, can help survivors to reclaim their connection to the Divine and re-narrate their experiences of suffering in light of this presence. Similarly, the Catholic emphasis on communion and the Church as the body of Christ can help to leverage the importance of community support for survivors as well. But this Catholic worldview is not always lived into, and the church has historically treated women as second-class members. Women remain barred from the top most leadership positions and this reality speaks volumes to both women and men. Boys and young men in the church begin to see themselves as privileged over women, laying the foundation for abusive behavior. And girls and women will not only see themselves as less than men, but as dependent on male voices in the church to speak to their concerns.

Theologian Denise Starkey points out the toxic reinforcement of gender stereotypes and patriarchal norms. For example, Pope John Paul II believed women to exercise their "feminine genius" in their capacity for motherhood and preservation of their virginity. We can see another misstep in the canonization of Maria Goretti, a young girl who was murdered by her attempted rapist, as the patron saint of youth and purity. As Starkey explains, "The implied assumption is that Maria chose death over impure desires. The emphasis on Maria's voluntary sacrifice indicates that it is better to die rather than endure the shame and humiliation of the loss of her virginity."[66] But ultimately, Starkey argues that the Catholic church can be a place of healing, "based on the awareness that a greater depth of resources exist within the Catholic spiritual tradition than many may know. Many women who object to the Church's stances on women continue to be Catholic because they affirm that church—the people of

---

65. USCCB, "When I Call for Help," 11.

66. Starkey, "The Roman Catholic Church," 183.

God—transcends institutional structures."[67] Starkey, along with many feminist Catholic theologians call the church to respond more fully to the issue of domestic violence and to create a preferential option for women and children in the Catholic church.

White Mainline Protestant Churches

White mainline Protestant churches, who trace their origins to European religious communities who left the Roman Catholic Church in the Middle Ages and are distinct from Black, fundamentalist, evangelical, and charismatic churches, also struggle with the Christian tradition's roots in the Roman household and practices of gender oppression. Minister and professor of pastoral counseling, Ron Clark, points to the history of misogyny in the church as the source of the hyper-masculinization of men and the hyper-feminization of women found in the Protestant church community today. He points to several resulting trends in the church, including a focus on two-parent households, aversions to modern women's rights and empowerment movements, the growth of a "spiritually based" health and beauty industry, a complicated relationship with LGBT rights, and a general anti-divorce stance taken by many pastors and congregants. Many of these trends are also empowered by a lack of critical engagement with scripture. Clark argues that the church must always work to interpret scripture to justify peace rather than violence, pointing to the liberative story of the Exodus as an important resource for pastors and congregations looking to scripture for wisdom in addressing domestic violence.[68]

Latino Protestant Churches

A growing community within the US Protestant church are Latinos, who are the largest ethnic minority group in the US. The identifying term "Latino" can be problematically simplifying, and is often applied to people from completely different countries of origin. But a shared history of Spanish and Portuguese conquest and colonization in Latin America has resulted in many cultural similarities across Central and South Americas. While the majority of Latinos in the United States are Catholic

67. Starkey, "The Roman Catholic Church," 184.
68. Clark, "Is There Peace within Our Walls?"

(68 percent), there is a smaller subsection that identifies as evangelical Protestant.[69] Many Latino Protestant churches have their roots in evangelizing US missionaries of the nineteenth-century, with many Protestant churches in Latin America originating as church plants of these missionaries. But since then, a growing portion of Latino Protestant churches are new denominations. And in the US, many of these Latino evangelical Protestants are converts from Catholicism, citing a wish for a more direct experience with God and animated church services as some of the reasons for their conversion.[70]

Like all religious communities, the Latino Protestant church is an important resource for survivors of domestic violence, but has also historically acted to disenfranchise women. The Latino Protestant church is naturally influenced by the cultural norms of the Latino community as a whole, the most significant in regards to domestic violence being Latino gender-roles. The female ideal of *marianismo*, originating from the Catholic veneration of the Virgin Mary, emphasizes submission, virginity, and the self-sacrifice of motherhood. The male ideal of *machismo* emphasizes dominance, honor, responsibility, and independence. Studies have shown that these strict gender divisions can result in toxic interpretations of intimate partner relationships, even to the point of marital rape.[71] Uncritical biblical interpretations (which we explored above) and Latino clergy and leadership, who are predominantly male and often lack any insight or training on the realities of domestic violence, exacerbate these cultural trends.

On the other hand, the cultural value of *familismo* emphasizes the importance of a strong and safe nuclear family and can help to reinforce more liberative interpretations of scripture and tradition. Sociologists Natalie Ames and Leslie F. Ware argue that the Latino Protestant church must work to develop resources for both survivors and perpetrators in their churches. For survivors, church response must acknowledge the dangers of remaining in an abusive relationship. And for perpetrators, churches can provide accountability and counseling, which both acknowledges the daily injustices Latino men face "and emphasize that oppression is not an excuse for abusive behavior."[72]

---

69. Pew Research Center, *Changing Faiths.*

70. Pew Research Center, *Changing Faiths.*

71. Perilla, "Domestic Violence as a Human Rights Issue."

72. Ames and Ware, "Latino Protestants."

African Ancestry Churches

Church communities of African Ancestry (African, African Caribbean, and African American) have long acted as central sources for economic, spiritual, physical, and social empowerment for Black Americans. Since its beginnings in the hush harbors, Black churches have worked for social and racial justice. But the Black church has not been as consistent in its stance on issues of gender, or specifically domestic violence. The Black community in the US, like the Latino community, is far from monolithic. The diversity of cultural backgrounds, including African, African Caribbean, and African American, is one reason why individual churches and their responses to domestic violence are so important. Each individual church community is more capable of addressing domestic violence through the lens of their community's cultural and spiritual makeup. Unfortunately, the embattled identity of these communities often means that violence against women takes a back seat to other social issues such as immigration, focus on the homeland, assimilation, racial injustice, the legacy of slavery, and others. In addition, the role of the church as a safe-haven for the Black community makes it complicated for the church to hold abusers accountable and reluctant to involve outside untrusted parties, such as the legal system.

According to sociologists Tricia Bent-Goodley and Kesslyn Brade Stennis, there are several commonalities across Black churches and spiritualities that act as compounding variables in these churches' response to domestic violence. These commonalities include a "recognition and reliance upon God, the horizontal and vertical nature of spirituality, the significance of community, and the traditional view surrounding gender roles."[73] These are all supported and interpreted using sacred texts, specifically the Bible. Each of these components of Black church spirituality have the ability to help or harm survivors of domestic violence depending on a number of factors such as the intent of spiritual leaders, levels of awareness around the issue of domestic violence, and personal histories. Similar to the other denominations and Christian traditions we have looked at in this section, the Black church has an opportunity to respond more fully to domestic violence, leveraging the tools and resources of its tradition for the flourishing of both survivors and abusers in its community.

73. Bent-Goodley and Stennis, "Intimate Partner Violence."

Rural Church Communities

The rural church also poses a unique context for engaging domestic violence. Nineteen percent of the US lives in low-density population areas, known as rural communities. These communities are generally close-knit enclaves, suspicious of newcomers or outsiders, shaped by high rates of poverty. These communities also have higher rates of religiosity and religious affiliation. Rural churches tend to be more conservative and fundamentalist forms of Christianity, practicing literal biblical interpretation. As seen above, more fundamentalist forms of biblical interpretation can lead to the reinforcement of strict gender roles and the ostracization of divorced or separated women. This, combined with the stigmatization of mental health and the value of self-sufficiency, often leaves survivors in rural churches believing they are responsible in some way for the abuse they are experiencing. Psychologists Donald F. Walker, Katherine J. Partridge, and Rachel L. Stephens point out that many therapists working with survivors in rural communities conflate their experiences of abuse and suffering with punishment from God for sins of the past.[74] But the all-encompassing nature of religiosity and the rural church also makes them powerful allies in helping survivors and perpetrators in these communities.

White Evangelical and Fundamentalist Churches

White Evangelical and Fundamentalist churches also play important roles for their communities as resources for support for both survivors and perpetrators, but can do more preventative work. Evangelical and Fundamentalist Christians are not synonymous, but they do overlap and include denominations such as Presbyterians, Congregationalists, Churches of Christ, the Church of the Nazerene, some Baptist congregations, as well as some nondenominational churches, and others. They also share several core values, including the strong authority of scripture in matters of faith and practice. While Fundamentalists believe in the inerrancy of the word of God, Evangelicals are more critical in their interpretation. Both churches have a heavy emphasis on the importance of conversion for salvation, which is possible through the atonement of sin through Jesus the Christ. This leads both communities to engage in public

74. Walker et al., "Addressing Intimate Partner Violence."

and counter-cultural practices of evangelism. Evangelicals tend to participate more fully in US culture than Fundamentalist, but both generally oppose gay and lesbian marriage, abortion, divorce, and premarital sex. Similarly, both are proponents of "traditional" family values, with Fundamentalist churches being strictly patriarchal. These trends and practices of women's submission within families coupled with other religious practices such as the value placed on forgiveness can make it difficult for survivors in these communities to leave their abusers. While fear of judgment from one's church community can be a barrier for survivors to leave an abusive relationship, scientists correlate positive religious coping within or after abuse with decreased traumatic symptoms. Therefore, it is important that Evangelical and Fundamentalist churches leverage their spiritual resources, train clergy on the prevalence of domestic violence, and take preventative measures in their communities to condemn abuse within families.[75]

Pentecostal and Charismatic Churches

Some denominations have more liberative roots than others. The founders of Pentecostalism, for example, focused on the egalitarian principles of the non-discriminatory nature of the Holy Spirit and the counter-cultural shifts of the Pentecost event. As the largest Protestant denominations, and the second largest Christian group (behind Roman Catholicism) globally, the Pentecostal church has access to and influence over many Christians in the US. The Pentacoastal church is defined by the belief that through baptism of the Holy Spirit, Christians may receive spiritual gifts such as prophecy, speaking in tongues, or faith healings. Charismatic churches are similar in that they have adopted these practices of spiritual gifts, but come from different denominations (i.e. Charismatic Catholics). Modern day Pentecostal churches trace their heritage to the outpouring of the Holy Spirit at the 1906 Azusa Street Revival, where African American preacher William J. Seymour began to speak in tongues, sparking a global movement. The early Pentecostal church believed God reformed society and humanity through baptism (and the Holy Spirit), creating an equality across gender and race within the church. The involvement of abolitionists, pacifists, and women's rights activists marked the first several decades of the Pentecostal church. By the 1930s, women

75. Stephens, and Walker, " Addressing Intimate Partner Violence."

had established over half of the existing Pentacostal congregations. Early on, the Pentecostal community encouraged women to reject traditional gender-roles and lead as equal members in the church.

Unfortunately, by mid-century the Pentecostal church's practices towards women began to shift, mirroring the gender-roles of growing Evangelical influences. The Pentecostal church shares the belief that the Bible is the central authority on matters of faith with the Evangelical church, and naturally these communities began to overlap. As seen above, scripture interpreted uncritically can be dangerous for addressing issues of domestic violence. Today, many Pentecostal writers and theologians continue to interpret scripture in light of the egalitarian message of Jesus and Pentecost. Authors, like J. Lee Grady, engage issues of domestic violence and marital equality through scriptural interpretations read through the lens of Christ's victory over death and sin and the renewal of society, where all are equal in the eyes of God.[76]

Anabaptist and Mennonite Churches

Falling neither in the Catholic nor Protestant categories, peace churches, such as Anabaptist, Mennonites, and Quakers, provide a unique response to domestic violence, focusing on practices of restorative justice. The different denominations of peace churches share practices such as nonviolence, forgiveness, reconciliation, and social justice. Naturally, a radically non-violent church community would denounce domestic violence, but the unique central role of the community in these traditions provides an interesting critique to the most common responses to domestic violence. By focusing on restorative justice in the aftermath of domestic violence, peace churches look to include the survivor, the abuser, and the community in the larger healing work. The inclusion of both survivor and abuser in the justice process, or conjoint intervention, is generally not considered best practice in the world of domestic violence response. There are concerns for the safety and health of the survivor, accountability of the perpetrator, and the possibility of ignoring larger cultural influences. But psychologist Peter Jankowski argues that this peace church practice can help address the varietal types of domestic violence and partners, and lead to overall better mental health and outcomes for all involved. In addition, the peace church traditions leverage the practices of forgiveness

---

76. Murphy et al., "Pentecostal and Charismatic Churches."

as part of the justice process. Survivors and advocates often recoil at the theological idea of forgiveness, because it is one theme often used by abusers to continue their cycles of abuse. But Jankowski notes that psychologically the practice of "unforgiveness" can have detrimental effects on the survivor. Therefore, it is important that we do not dismiss these practices, but rather critically engage them for their potential in healing communities.[77]

Can the Christian Church Be a Place of Healing?

Do the possibilities of healing and transformation found within these Christian traditions above offset thousands of years of enabling and perpetrating abuse? Some feminist theologians and scholars question the possibility of saving the tradition from this difficult history of authorizing violence against women. We must ask the question, put forward by Joanne Carlson Brown and Carole R Bohn, "Is it possible to be a feminist and retain some attachment to the Christian tradition?" And once we complete the exorcism, "can we call our 'corrected' Christianity Christianity?"[78] There are some feminist scholars, such as Joanna Carlson Brown and Rebecca Parker, who are skeptical. Brown and Parker argue that the Christian tradition is centrally founded on the glorified suffering of Jesus of Nazareth, an innocent victim, and therefore it is ultimately dangerous to the health of women who remain within this tradition. Christianity has argued that the death of Jesus on the cross is the central salvific moment for the world. By tracing the three most prominent Christian atonement theories (*Christus Victor*, satisfaction theory, and moral influence) and considering more modern theories (the suffering God, the necessity of suffering, and the negativity of suffering), Brown and Parker conclude that "We [women] have been convinced that our suffering is justified."[79] For these authors, regardless of the nuances that we may apply to these atonement theologies, the central claim that our salvation is an effect of the crucifixion of an innocent person is irredeemable. "The glorification of anyone's suffering allows the glorification of all suffering. To argue that salvation can only come through the cross is to

---

77. Jankowski, "An Anabaptist-Mennonite Perspective."

78. Brown and Bohn, "Introduction," xiii–xv.

79. Brown and Parker, "For God So Loves the World?" 36.

make God a divine sadist and a divine child abuser."[80] Therefore, Brown and Parker argue, women *must* leave the Church in order to live and those who stay to work from within are living as victims in an abusive relationship and essentially trying to change an abusive partner.[81]

But there are feminist theologians, such as Rosemary Radford Ruether among many others, who do stay within the tradition to fight for women's rights, equality, and flourishing. Radford Ruether argues against Brown and Parker's claim that the glorification of innocent suffering is the core of salvation in Christianity. Radford Ruether writes that "Christianity has in it the seeds of an alternative theory, a theory of liberation, equality, and dignity for all persons. But this idea has seldom been applied to women in the religious tradition, either historically or today."[82] It is this seed of "liberation, equality, and dignity for all persons" for which feminist theologians have fought, researched, written, and lived. It is this often-neglected seed of hope and healing with which this book is centrally concerned.

Moving the Conversation Forward

"To hold traumatic reality in consciousness requires a social context that affirms and protects the victim and that joins victim and witness in a common alliance. For the individual victim, this social context is created by relationships with friends, lovers, and family. For the larger society, the social context is created by political movements that give voice to the disempowered."

JUDITH HERMAN[83]

After the feminist theological work of the 1990s, many feminist theologians engaging questions of suffering and violence turned to the lens of trauma theory. Integrating the discussions and research outlined above, feminist trauma theologians, such as Jennifer Beste, Flora Keshgegian, and Serene Jones, looked at the theological problems posed by traumatic experiences like sexual abuse and domestic violence. In the same vein as earlier feminist, these theologians have stepped into a critical

80. Brown and Parker, "For God So Loves the World?" 53.

81. Brown and Parker, "For God So Loves the World?" 37–38.

82. Radford Ruether, "The Western Religious Tradition," 40.

83. Herman, *Trauma and Recovery*, 9.

role of deconstructing and reconstructing our theological understandings in light of suffering, violence, and trauma. While feminist trauma theologians have continued to bring the theological conversation about domestic violence forward, the conversation cannot stop with applying theological language to the problem of trauma or psychological language to the field of theology. Just as medical professionals, psychologists, and sociologists helped to give language to the mental health problems experienced by survivors and communities affected by domestic violence, theologians writing about trauma and domestic violence help to give theological language to the spiritual problems experienced by those same communities.

Domestic violence poses a particular theological problem because it threatens the agency of survivors and their ability to connect with others on a fundamental level. Personal agency and connection to a community are central aspects of many important theological ideas, particularly around questions of grace, salvation, healing, and transformation. For example, Jennifer Beste interrogates Karl Rahner's theology of freedom in light of the experiences of incest survivors. Karl Rahner's theology of freedom argues that within our human freedom we possess all that is necessary to choose God's grace. Beste, drawing from her experience of working with incest survivors, argues that the trauma survivor's experiences inhibit their ability to choose grace and therefore there is an aspect of grace that is socially mediated. For this reason, it is only through supportive relationships with others that we can access our true relationship with the Divine.[84] Beste's understanding of grace as mediated through others is significant for incest survivors because it places the burden of mediation on the community as a whole rather than the individual, who may or may not be able to relate to themselves in that type of manner.

In addition to helping to rebuild agency, the community also plays a role in remembering and naming the abuse, an important step in the healing process. Another feminist trauma theologian, Flora Keshgegian, also working from the context of survivors of childhood abuse, turns to the community's role in helping name and acknowledge the strength of survivors in the practice of "re-membering." Keshgegian focuses on re-membering as a central part of healing for survivors and communities. By naming and claiming moments of hope and survival amidst situations of trauma, survivors and their communities move forward in the healing

84. Beste, *God and the Victim*, 101.

process. Keshgegian argues that the Church is the central example of this type of "community of remembrance and witness" and unpacks a number of the Church's functions and practices in light of this role.[85]

The community's role of remembering requires imagination. For feminist trauma theologian Serene Jones, the formation of imagination becomes a central role for theology. Jones argues that "theology's task is to renarrate to us what we have yet to imagine."[86] In this way, theological imagination provides a significant resource for trauma healing. Jones argues that grace can reshape our imaginations after trauma, but theological language and relationships are what mediate that grace for survivors of violence. The task of theology is to help survivors to tell, witness, and retell their stories anew.[87] This, in effect, is the reordering of our imaginations. To illustrate this point, Jones uses the scriptural example of Emmaus.

Two disciples are on their way to Emmaus in the days after witnessing the crucifixion. Jones describes their state as disordered and traumatized, when the risen Jesus joins them. Because of their disordered state, they do not recognize him. They talk together along the road, but it is not until they stop and share a meal together that the disciples recognize him in the ritual breaking of the bread. Jones writes, "In this simple ritual action, memory is sparked—a lost truth recalled—and suddenly their eyes are opened, and they recognize him."[88] The practice of communion, through grace, provided the disciples with a way to reorder their imagination and understand their trauma in a different way. In this example, the disciples understood Jesus as risen, rather than still dead, after the communal meal and reconnecting as a community. For Jones, our imagination and ability to reorder our understanding of our experiences using the theological tools and schema provided by the Christian tradition ground our ability to move forward after trauma.

Beste, Keshgegian, Jones, and other feminist trauma theologians all highlight the importance of community in the healing journey of trauma survivors. Their work not only pushes the theological conversation towards a dialogue between the experience of trauma and theology, but also begins to point towards practical responses and possible paths of

85. See Keshgegian, *Redeeming Memories*, 200.

86. Jones, *Trauma and Grace*, 21.

87. Jones, *Trauma and Grace*, 33.

88. Jones, *Trauma and Grace*, 40.

healing. So how do survivors of domestic violence heal within communities? And what does that communal healing in turn tell us about our theologies of salvation, hope, and resurrection? In order to answer these questions and further understand the healing work of survivors, I turn to the stories and experiences of a particular community of domestic violence survivors at the House of Peace.

Feminist trauma theologians often situate their theological inquiries within particular communities affected by trauma, violence, and suffering. For example, both Jennifer Beste and Flora Keshgegian work with survivors of child sexual abuse. The particular context and types of trauma experienced impact the theological questions being considered. In this book, I hope to continue this contextualization of trauma and theology further, highlighting the effects and importance of race and class, in addition to gender and life experience. By turning to the experiences and voices of Latina survivors at the Chicago domestic violence shelter, House of Peace, I explore the nuances and intricacies of trauma healing as experienced in a particular context and their implications for our theologies of hope. The significance of race and class have traditionally been ignored by white feminist and trauma theorists. While allowing authors to make broader universal claims about the human experience, trauma, and healing, the absence of race and class as contextual themes have often resulted in the assumption of a white middle-class subject, remaining blind to the particular problems and wisdoms of communities of color.

In this book, I approach domestic violence as a theological problem that has the possibility of reshaping both our theologies and practices of hope, as situated in particular contexts, beyond the one-way application of theology to domestic violence. The principle of sacramentality grounds this method. As Catholic feminist scholar Susan Abraham writes, "Thus, it is not just the sacraments that are sacramental. Reality itself is sacramental because God chooses to relate to reality."[89] In the context of this book, the reality and experiences of practices of healing after domestic violence become possible sacramental sites, meaning the practices and narratives of the domestic violence survivors at House of Peace become imaginable sites of divine presence through which we can further discover the human-Divine relationship and God's role in our healing and daily lives.

89. Abraham, "Justice as the Mark," 197.

Domestic violence is a theological problem that affects survivors' and communities' ability to practice hope, because domestic violence disrupts our agency, connection to others, and our ability to imagine a different future. Therefore, communities of survivors of domestic violence that are able to create and practice hope help us to re-imagine our theological concepts, narratives, and practices of hope in light of trauma healing. We experience hope as both an attitude about the openness of the future and a commitment to bringing that future world about. Hope implies not only imagining the possibility of the self and others to live into an ideal future, but also the bodily, communal practices that incarnate that future. Feminist and trauma theologians' writings have long pointed to the theological challenges domestic violence poses, diagnosing it as a theological problem. In this book, I hope to take these conversations forward, looking at the theological challenges posed by domestic violence to the theology and practice of hope.

Practices of hope cultivate the flourishing of life, restoring individual and communal agency, opening the future, and providing pathways to obtain that future. What hope practices look like are always tied to particular places and times. Hope takes on different forms defined by the situation of the individual and community who experience suffering. Therefore, the practices and concepts of hope are not universal. In this respect, the practices that embody hope now or for one group, may not in the future or for a different group. If hope is this mercurial, what is the purpose of its study? Keshgegian writes that "A modesty of hope does not make hope any less compelling, any less necessary. Indeed, it has the opposite effect. Our hope is quite intensified in the moment, whichever moment, in which we live."[90] Keshgegian points to a postmodern hope that is modest and situational. More than just an "optimistic" outlook on the future, the contextual hope that Keshgegian develops and I engage in this book is shaped by the bodies that practice it, the minds that imagine it, and the communities that bring it into reality. With this in our minds, I ask the question, "What constitutes hope after domestic violence?"

90. Keshgegian, *Time for Hope*, 182.

3

Women's Suffering, Salvation, and the Empty Tomb

THE EXPERIENCES AND NARRATIVES of domestic violence survivors shine a spotlight on the evils which lurk below the surface of our society. Today, we are witnessing a public reckoning in the United States and globally in regards to these evils, including rape culture, gender and racial inequality, and economic disparity. But without listening to the voices of those who have suffered under the systemic evils of our culture, we risk misdiagnosing the problems and, as a result, our solutions will fall short. Our conversations on what healing looks like in our context must place narratives that speak to survivors of domestic violence at the center. One such narrative, the vindication of the Suffering One, is an account found throughout the Judaeo-Christian tradition, and shapes how we talk about suffering and healing today. Specifically, the shorter ending of Mark, known as the Empty Tomb, is a portrayal of how early Jesus followers interpreted Jesus' death and resurrection in the wake of the Jewish War and the destruction of the temple. This original ending is unique from other Gospel resurrection narratives because Jesus does not appear. Rather the trauma of the crucifixion remains even though God vindicates Jesus, as announced in the narrative by the young man in the tomb. In this chapter, I argue that the Empty Tomb narrative can help make sense of healing after domestic violence. The narrative's traumatic context and undertone, in addition to its examples of practices of resistance and discipleship, all help to present a picture of fragile resurrection. In the next chapter, dialogue with survivors of domestic violence will deepen these unique aspects of the Empty Tomb.

In the first chapter, we explored the role of context in shaping how we practice and understand hope. In this chapter, I will carry the importance of context forward to the theological ideas of suffering and salvation.[1] Suffering and salvation, represented by the cross and resurrection in the earliest of Christian narratives, are deeply interconnected and part of a single narrative framework.[2] Experiences of suffering shape the ways in which Christians speak of healing and salvation. Salvation is understood in the particular context of suffering that is experienced. The grounding question of this book— "What and where is hope after domestic violence?"—requires that we explore the context of both suffering and healing from domestic violence. In this chapter, I will outline a feminist exegesis of the Gospel of Mark's Empty Tomb narrative and trace the expansion of the crucifixion and resurrection by several feminist Latina theologians. In the following chapter, I will then bring the narratives of a particular community of domestic violence survivors into the conversation, culminating in a re-imagining and deepening of the Empty Tomb narrative as told through the suffering and healing experiences of Latina domestic violence survivors at House of Peace.

The Gospel of Mark's Empty Tomb

The Gospel of Mark is a story of trauma with world-ending implications. While scholars debate the historical context of the Markan author and community, what is clear is the author intended this narrative of Jesus' life, death, and resurrection for an audience on an apocalyptic edge. Dated by most scholars to around 70 CE, the author of Mark was writing for an audience who had experienced the end of their world, the destruction of the Jewish Temple. The author intended Jesus' death and resurrection, told through the narrative framing of the Suffering and Vindication of the Innocent One, to not only reflect the audience's own experience of loss and persecution under the Roman Empire, but to also tie their

1. For the purpose of this chapter, I use the word salvation to refer to the healing and unification with God that takes place after trauma within history. In this particular book, I am not intending to develop a full eschatological picture of salvation, but I am aware that my claims about salvation in the here and now certainly have implications for the eschaton. These will have to be fleshed out in other works.

2. The inspirational source material for this narrative comes from the larger tradition of the Suffering Innocent One. See Nickelsburg, "Resurrection, Immortality, and Eternal Life"; and Dewey, *Inventing the Passion*, 71–73.

fate with that of Jesus' resurrection.[3] And yet, what strikes most scholars about this passage is the "un-ending." The earliest ending to Mark is surprisingly absent of a risen Jesus. "This ending only faintly anticipated the resurrection, still preserving some of the sting of the traumatic loss of Jesus."[4] The later endings of Mark include appearances of Jesus to the disciples, but most scholars agree these were added by other authors.[5] As the Gospel of Mark aged and its audience shifted from the immediate crisis, others may have added these endings to make sense of the fact that the world actually didn't end.

In the oldest ending of Mark (Mark 16:1–8), the author focuses our attention on three women disciples, who are planning to anoint the body of Jesus as part of preparation for burial. Mary Magdalene, Mary mother of James, and Salome leave their homes at first light after the Sabbath has ended. On their way, they discuss how they will have to move the large stone, which was in front of the tomb. Once they are in front of the tomb, they find the stone is missing and a young man in white robes is waiting inside. Inside the tomb, the young man announces Jesus' resurrection to the women, telling them he has gone ahead of them to Galilee. The young man also instructs the women to tell the other disciples. Then the oldest ending of Mark finishes with the women fleeing the tomb in "terror and amazement," saying nothing to anyone.

This original ending of Mark, with its lack of physical appearance by Jesus, seems incomplete for some readers. Some theologians, such as Job Sobrino, feel that this original ending lacks the hope found in other appearance focused narratives. Sobrino places the significance of the resurrection later in the tradition, when the disciples overcome their doubts and receive their missional charge.[6] Sobrino, uncomfortable with the ambiguity of the original ending to Mark, follows in the footsteps of later gospel writers and moves quickly past the Empty Tomb, wanting to guard against disbelief, hopelessness, and misinterpretation. The problem with this reading of the Empty Tomb is that it misses the historical context from which Mark's Gospel comes. Because the narrative mirrors the Suffering Innocent One, the Gospel's audience would have connected the dots between Jesus' death and resurrection and their own fates. The

3. See Nickelsburg, *Resurrection, Immortality, and Eternal Life*; and Dewey, *Inventing the Passion*, 71–73.

4. Carr, *Holy Resilience*, 231.

5. Billings, "The End of Mark's Gospel and the Markan Community," 44.

6. Sobrino, *Christ the Liberator*, 56–57.

announcement from the young man signals that God, who is just, has accepted Jesus, the innocent one, and all those throughout history who suffer unjustly. In dismissing this account, we lose a tradition that speaks particularly to a context of trauma and our current moment of apocalyptic anxiety.

Biblical feminist scholar Elisabeth Schüssler Fiorenza highlights other biblical scholars and a traditioon of unequal treatment between the "Empty Tomb tradition" and the later "appearances tradition." Schüssler Fiorenza refers to these two as the female and male traditions, respectively. She has been criticized for this labeling, but argues that scholars separate these traditions in similarly constructed ways to gender's construction.[7] Unfortunately, scholars have historically considered the gender of the witnesses in both accounts a major factor in their level of authority. Privileging accounts that include male disciples and the presence of the authoritative figure of Jesus, scholars have often overlooked the female disciples at the center of the Empty Tomb account.[8] Instead of a physical appearance, the young man announces the resurrection and the women, as well as the audience, are left to make sense of this message. Feminist biblical scholars, such as Mary Rose D'Angelo, Schüssler Fiorenza, and Carolyn Oseik, bring the Empty Tomb tradition back into the theological conversation.[9]

Along with the lack of appearance by the risen Christ, many scholars contemplate the author's reasoning behind ending the narrative with the three women fleeing the tomb in terror, amazement, and silence. Some biblical scholars, such as Bradley Billings, argue that the author of Mark left the ending "unsaid" because of the radical and subversive nature of Jesus' resurrection, as a signal of the end. Billings notes that the Markan community was an apocalyptic community and believed they were on the edge of the Parousia, marked by the overthrow of earthly rulers.[10] Another scholar, Marianne Sawicki, ties this narrative to the earliest ritualized practices of Hellenized Jewish women mourning and memorializing

7. O'Collins and Kendall, "Mary Magdalene"; and Schüssler Fiorenza, *Jesus*, 124.

8. In example, Catholic scholar William Portier referred to the Empty Tomb tradition as a "subordinate or subsidiary 'sign' of the resurrection" in his systematic work *Tradition & Incarnation* (346), because of Paul's silence on the account and its seeming weakness in testimony compared to the other appearance accounts.

9 See works such as D'Angelo, *Women and Christian Origins*, Schüssler, *Jesus*; and Osiek, "The Women at the Tomb."

10. Billings, "The End of Mark's Gospel and the Markan Community," 54.

the death of Jesus.[11] Scholar Joan Mitchell puts forth the thesis that "The narrative preserves the moment and suspends the women deliberately in wordless awe at this threshold."[12] Once the women speak the moment will pass. She argues that silence and fear are part of discipleship throughout Mark's Gospel and are not weaknesses tied to their female-ness, but rather their roles as disciples. Through the Gospel of Mark, the author portrays the disciples as failures, misunderstanding and ultimately abandoning Jesus. The disciples, as well as the women, are foils for the audience to compare their own knowledge and loyalty against.

Many scholars have pointed to this passage as proof of women's discipleship during the time of Jesus. The language used to describe the women as those who "followed" Jesus echo the language used to talk about the male disciples.[13] The presence of the women at the tomb and the absence of the male disciples has often been held up as a case for the strength of female disciples. "In Mark, the unnamed women at the cross serve a double narrative function: they provide witnesses to the reality of Jesus' death and underline the failure of the male disciples, who have fled."[14] This line of thinking can open up female discipleship to critique. If this story is read as a tale of women's exceptionalism in discipleship, it can also be read as a tale of their ultimate failure, because the passage ends with their silence.[15] Also, as we discussed earlier, the disciples in Mark are not positive examples of what the author believes discipleship should be and through their failures the audience understands the author's true intentions for them.

Rather than a direct representation of women in the life of Jesus, the Empty Tomb can be re-imagined in light of Mark's understanding of discipleship. The women at the tomb are unique from the male disciples in Mark's narrative because of their loyalty, bravery, and solidarity with the crucified. The women choose to be present at the crucifixion and at the tomb, where they are the first to witness the announcement of his resurrection. Throughout Mark's Gospel, the author ties discipleship to loyalty, even in the face of suffering, what Schüssler Fiorenza calls, "suffering discipleship." Schüssler Fiorenza argues that Mark depicts discipleship as

11. Sawicki, "Making Jesus," 163–65.

12. Mitchell, *Beyond Fear and Silence*, 2.

13. De'Angelo, "Unnamed Women at the Cross," 437. See also Schüssler Fiorenza, *In Memory of Her*, 316–23.

14. De'Angelo, "Unnamed Women at the Cross," 438.

15. Fowler, *Let the Reader Understand*, 89.

a radical solidarity with Christ and the crucified of history. The author calls us to be in solidarity with those who suffer, which the women at the Empty Tomb fully embody by risking their lives and well-being to accompany Jesus' body to the tomb.[16] This is far from a call to suffering obedience. And if the author intends discipleship to be a glorified self-sacrifice, we must engage this critically. Rather, Schüssler Fiorenze argues that suffering is not an end in itself, but the result of living a life of solidarity. Suffering discipleship is not equivalent with accepting abuse or oppression, or putting yourself in harm's way for the purpose of self-sacrifice. But rather, suffering is often the result of a discipleship of resistance against the powers of the oppressor in solidarity with the oppressed. The opposite of passive suffering, the women disciples enact agency in their choice to go to the Empty Tomb, intending to practice subversive funeral rituals, against the will of the Empire.

Mark's Empty Tomb is the end of a crucifixion and resurrection narrative, a narrative in which the powers that be reject the Suffering One, but God restores them. Theologians and practitioners have applied this narrative to our own lives throughout history for good and for bad. Sometimes these applications can be toxic, requiring self-sacrifice and passive obedience. These readings can be particularly problematic for survivors of domestic violence. Other times, this narrative becomes a call to resistance and a promise to those oppressed and rejected by this world, that God remembers us in our suffering and will restore us. In our search for hope after domestic violence, we first turn to the narrative of the cross and its insights for framing women's suffering.

From Jesus' Cross to the Crosses of "Being Born a Woman"

"A feminist theological perspective that looks beyond the crucifixion of one man for the salvation of all denounces using the cross to maintain the oppression of women and the poor."

IVONE GEBARA[17]

Latina feminist scholars understand the cross as a complex symbol, which is contradictory in itself. This idea is not new to the Christian tradition. In the Gospel of Mark, the cross used in Jesus' execution would

---

16. Schüssler Fiorenza, *In Memory of Her*, 316–23.

17. Gebara, *Out of the Depths*, 112–13.

have signaled the larger context of Roman oppression and the trauma the Markan audience experienced during The Jewish War. The cross, originally a tool of torture and extermination the Roman Empire used to consolidate power and erase dissidents, has also become a symbol of resurrection and salvation. The cross has been used to oppress peoples throughout history, but has also been at the center of Christian worship.[18] The cross can be a euphemism for all negative life events, at the same time as being uniquely connected to Jesus' death, specifically as the cross of an innocent person. Liberation theologian Ivone Gebara writes, "Jesus' suffering on the cross has often served as an excuse for justifying the misery imposed on the poor and especially on women,"[19] alluding to centuries of oppression justified by the possible salvific properties of such suffering. Not only has Christianity long struggled with the glorification of suffering as something that will make our faith stronger and bring us closer to God, but if Jesus, an innocent victim, experienced suffering on the cross, who are we to think we deserve otherwise?

But our conversation around the cross must evolve, and grow to incorporate the complex experiences of suffering throughout history, including the experiences of modern day Latina survivors of violence. Jesus' experience of crucifixion is only accessible to us through the Gospels, each shaped by their communities and authors, which is why we must look beyond this singular example of suffering. While the author of Mark constructed their Gospel account to mirror the Tale of the Suffering Innocent One in order to speak to the experience of the early Jesus followers in the traumatic wake of The Jewish War, we are in a new and different context. This narrative no longer functions in the same way. But by incorporating women's experience into the understanding of the cross, feminist theologians hope to exorcise the symbol of its oppressive uses and strengthen its ability to liberate women and others.

Jesus' sacrifice on the cross has become the exemplar of self-sacrifice and salvific suffering. The problem of suffering and evil has been a central concern for theologians throughout history. But over the past half century, feminist theologians have brought women's suffering more prominently into the theological conversation. The suffering of women, explored in Gebara's work, *Out of the Depths*, comes in physical, psychological, and social forms, and often occurs in the private sphere of our society. This layered suffering women experience is certainly true

18. Gebara, *Out of the Depths*, 112.

19. Gebara, *Out of the Depths*, 112–13.

of Latina domestic violence survivors today, who face marginalization from the public sphere as immigrant women and experience the private sphere as abusive. Our society and their families deny them rights and justice. We often consider the litany of suffering experienced by wives, widows, mothers, daughters, sisters, prostitutes, slaves, and others to be unavoidable facts of women's private lives. While we push the suffering of women to the margins of society, making it invisible, and consider it un-important or inconsequential, "male forms" of suffering take the form of public acts of heroism and sacrifice, and ultimately are considered more meaningful.[20] Ironically and despite his passivity in death, Jesus' death on a cross has become the central Christian example of public male suffer-ing, leaving women's experiences of suffering disconnected from both the cross and the following resurrection.[21]

The silence and lack of public response surrounding women's suf-fering is also true of domestic violence. Violence and abuse within the private realm of the home has long been a daily experience for women. Abuse experienced at the hands of a loved one has been a normal part of life for women and has remained legal and supported by the dominant cultures of our world throughout most of history. Our global history of patriarchy and empire has long resulted in women, along with other disenfranchised groups and classes, carrying the bulk of the burden of suffering in this world and makes the consideration of Latina, immigrant women's suffering integral to the theological conversations on the cross. Despite the historical over-emphasis on the maleness of Jesus, Christian women have often identified with the cross, Jesus' suffering, and the gos-pel message. In her interviews and work with women from a poor area of Brazil, Gebara heard descriptions of the cross of "being born a female." In societies that have patriarchal roots, which unfortunately has been the dominant reality around the world for most of history, much of the suffering women experience is a result of "being born a female." Gebara reflects, "for them, the cross was not just the suffering of their daily lives in poverty but also their condition as women. The popular, patriarchal versions of Christianity taught them to bear and even welcome their cross rather than to look for a way to be rid of it."[22]

20. Gebara, *Out of the Depths.*
21. Gebara, *Out of the Depths,* 111.
22. Gebara, *Out of the Depths,* 113.

Nancy Pineda-Madrid's work with the community in Ciudad Juárez, Mexico uncovers a similar cross for those who are unlucky enough to be "born female." In her theological work, Pineda-Madrid confronts the experience of the women and families, who live with the systematic killing of their young women, orchestrated by gang-members and corrupted officials. Pineda-Madrid witnesses the use of pink crosses by the community of Ciudad Juárez in both vigils and protests for the victims of the mass violence in that city. Perpetrators focus their violence against the women, especially younger, poor women, who gangs and others target because of their gender and inability to retaliate due to their class. The pink crosses subvert the often masculine understanding of the cross in this community, connecting the systematic killings of these young women with the death and suffering of Jesus. Pineda Madrid refers to the crosses and other such practices as "practices of resistance."[23] The pink crosses, representing the suffering and death of the local women in Juárez, connect a particular experience of suffering, shame, and humiliation with the story of Jesus and the symbol of the cross. Just as the author of Mark connects their audience's experience to the Suffering Innocent One through the narrative of Jesus crucifixion and resurrection, the pink crosses connect the murdered women to each other and other victims of history. "Through their reinterpretation of the Christian symbol of the cross, the creators of the practices of resistance shine a spotlight on the relationship between female humanity and the possibility of salvation."[24]

Similar to Ignacio Ellacuría and Jon Sobrino's "crucified peoples," as well as the Markan author's own intentions in connecting his audiences through Jesus with all innocent sufferers, Gebara and Pineda-Madrid work to extend the symbolic meaning of the cross beyond the person of Jesus. They connect the cross to contemporary contexts in a way that connects instances of suffering at the hands of patriarchy and the Empire to each other. This understanding of the cross, as multiple in representation to include the everyday suffering of women and all those victims of the Empire before and after Jesus, does not deny or forget Jesus' death on a cross, but rather extends its significance to a larger historical narrative. When Jesus' cross becomes the only cross, we risk glorifying it, holding it up as a distant and unattainable example of self-sacrifice and innocent suffering. Gebera talks about this risk in the language of the Empire. She

---

23. Pineda-Madrid, "Responding to Social Suffering."
24. Pineda-Madrid, *Suffering and Salvation*, 145.

writes that "One cross cannot contain all suffering or all crosses. It would risk founding an empire of suffering even if the end were to found the empire of love."[25] When Christians and theologians talk about the cross of Jesus as the "greatest of all suffering," they diminish or exclude other forms of suffering from the conversation. Gebara writes, "[Jesus' cross] surely represents a reference to a community of faith, but it must be set in dialogue with others if it is to avoid manipulation."[26] The manipulation is the systemic use of Jesus' cross to legitimize certain forms of sacrifice and suffering, which benefit the Empire, while also pushing other forms of suffering, especially the suffering of women out of theological consideration. The totalizing centrality of Jesus' cross in the Christian tradition, "absolutized on a theoretical and practical level, becomes a way to exclude other suffering."[27] In the exclusion of other particular crosses, such as the cross of "being born female" or domestic violence, we sever women's suffering from its connection to resurrection, salvation, and hope. "To cling to the cross of Jesus as the major symbol of Christianity ultimately affirms the path of suffering and male martyrdom as the only way to salvation and to highlight injustice toward women and humanity."[28]

"Clinging" to the cross of Jesus does not only silence women's everyday experiences of suffering in favor of male-focused public martyrdom, but it also risks overemphasizing the male-ness of Jesus. Throughout history, women's ability to represent Christ has been questioned because of gender.[29] Ironically, the Roman Empire intended the practice of crucifixion to emasculate and shame political prisoners. If women cannot represent Christ in their suffering, as christomorphic, then the crucifixion and resurrection of Jesus does not save women. Pineda-Madrid pushes this further, arguing that if women believe they are not equal to men in their ability to image Christ, "[w]omen have, then, less reason to place

---

25. Gebara, *Out of the Depths*, 120.

26. Gebara, *Out of the Depths*, 117.

27. Gebara, *Out of the Depths*, 117.

28. Gebara, *Out of the Depths*, 118.

29. Elizabeth Johnson critiques the Christian tradition's myopic concern with God and Jesus' male-ness, in her watershed feminist work, *She Who Is*. For Johnson, if women cannot also represent the body of Christ as christomorphic, then women are not a part of the divine work of salvation. She brings into question the universality of Jesus as a salvific symbol for the Christian tradition. For more see Johnson, *She Who Is*, 72.

their hope in the power of God to save them."[30] If the particular cross and resurrection of the male Jesus become the *only* experiences considered to be legitimate examples of suffering and salvation, then women risk losing their access to hope.

"Can a male savior save women?" Gebara tackles this question posed by feminist Rosemary Radford Ruether, by focusing on the relatedness and interdependence of all creation. If all of creation is completely interdependent then an individual event of salvation is deeply connected to all other events of salvation. Gebara includes men, women, and nature in this discussion, writing, "It would be possible to transcend the male symbolism of the body of Christ by introducing an image of Christ as salvation coming from men and women and nonhuman nature. This Christ would exist in Jesus of Nazareth but also beyond him."[31] But Gebara's expansion and turn to all of creation ignores the rich underlying textual tradition of The Suffering Innocent One we find in Mark's gospel narrative of Jesus' crucifixion. By turning to all of creation, Gebara seems to circumvent Jesus' death, rather than place it within its context. Women's suffering, along with the suffering of men and all of creation, connects to and echoes the cross of Jesus. Moments of resurrection follow these multitudes of crosses throughout history. Jesus' resurrection roots these resurrection events, but also goes far beyond that single historical moment.

From Jesus' Resurrection to the Resurrections of Women

As we extend the cross to new contexts, beyond that of Jesus of Nazareth, it multiplies. The current suffering of women is one such new context. There are crosses of suffering and oppression throughout history, all in different times and places. We do not speak of "a cross," nor do we restrict the resurrection to one episode in our theological reflections. Before returning to the specific narrative of the Empty Tomb, we turn to the works of theologians Gebara and Pineda-Madrid to extend the resurrection to the contextual experiences of women's salvation, in the same way they worked to extend the cross. Their work lays the foundation for us to label historical moments of healing "*resurrections*," or "resurrection-moments." The expansion of the resurrection beyond Jesus is possible because the cross and the resurrection are deeply interconnected. As the

30. Pineda-Madrid, *Suffering and Salvation*, 91.

31. Gebara, *Out of the Depths*, 143.

cross extends to the suffering of women, so extends the resurrection to the possibility of their healing.

The Fragility of Life and Redemption

The cross and resurrection duality reflects the contradictory and revelatory nature of our own lives. Musing on this dichotomy of our lives, Gebara writes "We live, as we know, a temporary succession of happy and sad events in our personal and collective existence."[32] The reality of life is that change is one of the only constants. We do not experience salvation once and for all, living the rest of human history without suffering, but neither is suffering all encompassing. Human history, and often our personal lives, ebbs and flows through times of violence, suffering, abuse, peace, salvation, and joy. Even abusive relationships themselves mirror this cycle; times of affection and care give way to escalation, control, and violence.

We can find the roots of our healing embedded in our moments of suffering, ready to grow and flower if we and our community nurture them. Gebara elaborates that "In the midst of trouble there is often the presence of neighbors and friends; often a member of the family or even some stranger is ready to help. Suffering is often mixed with solidarity, assistance, and understanding."[33] We can find our resources for healing in our darkest times. Often in our moments of exhaustion and weariness, those who come to provide comfort and support surprise us. These people and resources shift and change throughout our lives, resisting a one-size fits all approach to healing and salvation. If we hunger, we need sustenance. If we ache, we need relief. We heal and reconnect to the Divine in different ways throughout our lives, depending on our circumstance. Salvation is an evolving experience, reshaped by context, experience, and the particular crucifixion. The circumstantial nature of our ability to heal leads me to employ the language of "resurrection-moments," which questions the singularity of Jesus' resurrection and points to the multivariate options at our disposal.

Gebara uses the language of "fragile redemption" to highlight the repetition of salvific moments. Because we continue to hunger, thirst, feel pain, become exhausted and weary, experience broken-heartedness and

32. Gebara, *Out of the Depths*, 110.
33. Gebara, *Out of the Depths*, 114.

betrayal, we do not recover from these states once and for all. We must re-imagine our healing practices and needs—our understanding of resurrection—again and again in light of what we suffer from—our experiences of the crucifixion. As I disclosed in the introduction of this chapter, the aspects of salvation I am engaging in are those aspects of healing post-trauma within history, and not the specific eschatological implications. Suffering and violence are a part of our lived experience, and will always remain with us in some respect. Therefore, we must renew our practices of hope and understandings of salvation with each new experience. Gebara compares this understanding of salvation with quenching thirst. She writes "It is there like a glass of water that quenches thirst for the moment, but thirst comes again, sometimes stronger than before. . . No sooner [the hoped for salvation] comes then it is gone: it escapes, flying away to prepare another and another. This *fragile redemption* is what we find in the everyday life of every person."[34] We experience our lives as an oscillation between suffering and salvation. This "fragile redemption" is deeply connected to the precariousness of our lives and we must practice it over and over. Like life itself, we must maintain our healing with nutrients, exercise, and support. The fragility of this redemption is not related to a weakness of the experience, but rather signals a flexibility. We can apply the flexibility of "fragile redemption" to a multitude of scenarios, helping us to "prepare" for new situations and the possible return of suffering. We become more nimble in our response to suffering and open to new possibilities.

Just as everyday we choose to renew our commitments to ourselves and others, an expanded understanding of resurrection can renew our ability to respond creatively to suffering. My hunger and weariness is always different. Today, the nutrients of my last meal, the passing of time, and my activity level, all shape my hunger. The raging pandemic, police brutality, the fear of the fall semester, and my toddler's inability to sleep past five in the morning, all shape my weariness. The same fragility is true of all of us. Gebara reminds us that "In practice we must always begin again every day the search for salvation just as every day we have to begin again the actions of eating and drinking."[35] We consciously renew our salvation in every moment and seek a "fragile redemption" that we enflesh and experience in the here and now, without denying either the remaining

---

34. Gebara, *Out of the Depths*, 123; my emphasis.

35. Gebara, *Out of the Depths*, 123.

effects of suffering or the possible future return of suffering. "Fragile redemption" makes room for the presence of suffering and crucifixion in
the midst of salvation. Experiences of suffering shape and change those
who experience them. But these moments of healing cannot completely
erase the trauma experienced, or the memory of suffering.

Salvation's Rooting in History

In the same way that the author of Mark connected Jesus to the larger
narrative of the suffering and vindication of the Innocent One, theologians and practitioners contextualize and expand the resurrection beyond the single event of Jesus by incorporating new narratives of healing
into the tradition. For example, Gebara does this in her work on salvation
by turning to the voices of women within her community. We find salvation in tangible events and moments in our lives. "Salvation is a baby long
awaited or a love letter that brings us back to life, Salvation is beauty, a
garden on the earth where God walks."[36] Salvation is not something that
is locked away and sparingly rationed. Salvation is found in consciously
attending to ourselves and each other. And it is never past-tense. In the
same way that the cross of "being born female" exposes the widespread
reality of women's suffering, the examples of moments and events we
name as healing, joyful, or rejuvenating point us to the prevalence and
abundance of "resurrection-moments" in our lives. The testimonies of
survivors of domestic violence shine a light on our reality and the evils of
gender oppression. In this same way, the stories of recovery and joy of domestic violence survivors can illuminate the accessible resources of hope
and healing. Salvation is related to the instability of life. The sacramental
aspects of life allow us to find hope and healing in our everyday experiences. Therefore, theologians and practitioners can look to the healing
narratives of our communities in order to understand salvation.

An understanding of salvation that is present in our everyday experiences is radically more accessible than a salvation that is *only* witnessed
as a second hand story of the life events of a man who lived two-thousand
years ago. When theologians or other church authorities point to Jesus'
resurrection—an event that is strategically kept historically and contextually removed from us— as the sole source of our healing and recon-
nection with God, they make salvation a scarce commodity. You can

36. Gebara, *Out of the Depths*, 124.

control and use a commodity. When church teachings restrict salvation to specific historical moments and figures, it only serves the status quo. If salvation is an ongoing process of resurrection moments embedded in our lives, then all of us are active participants and have access to healing. In the words of Gebara, "Salvation will not be something outside the fabric of life but will take place within the heart of it."[37] An understanding of salvation that is not, in some capacity, connected to our embodied lives and experiences of suffering is empty theological jargon and not productive or healing.

A promise of a salvation that is completely outside of history creates an "optimistic" hope that does not produce action, but rather creates complacency. This shallow understanding of salvation pushes healing outside of history or to the end of history, taking the form of a disconnected afterlife. In this afterlife narrative, our lived experiences, choices, and historical participation do not affect salvation. Our joy and delight will be uniform, who and how we loved has no effect. The same food and comfort will sate my hunger and weariness as well as yours. Humanity can selfishly sit back and watch all of creation burn, because those who are "saved" are still rewarded, while the "unsaved" are punished. But this type of narrative ignores the work of justice and healing that we must engage in now, within history. Gebara writes, "Salvation is not primarily an abstract and universal idea that encompasses the whole world or only life after death. Salvation is for the daily routine both light and darkness, laughter and tears, in which our life unfolds."[38] When we expand salvation beyond Jesus' resurrection event, to our present-day experiences of healing, then we become agents of change and justice.

Working for Salvation through Justice

While "resurrection-moments" are abundant and accessible, they do require us to consciously work. Salvation is not passive, but rather necessitates human action. "The issue is to recognize that the salvation experienced by Jesus, as well as or own salvation, does not occur automatically through the cross imposed by an imperial power but through promoting relationships of justice, respect, and tenderness among human beings."[39]

37. Gebara, *Out of the Depths*, 121.
38. Gebara, *Out of the Depths*, 127.
39. Gebara, *Out of the Depths*, 113.

Mark's construction of the passion narrative reflects this. The author connects Jesus to the suffering and vindication of the Innocent One to highlight God's approval of Jesus' teachings of justice and love. The audience of Mark would have understood the narrative of Jesus' death and resurrection, and the failure of the disciples, as a call to live into a true discipleship of solidarity. When theologians and practitioners reframe the work of salvation as taking place now and in history, rather than reserved to a single moment in time or the afterlife, our passivity towards injustice is no longer tolerable. The urgency of our contexts call us to *work* towards justice and salvation.

Practices that work towards justice and salvation are acts of hope. As I outlined in the first chapter, a productive hope practice works towards a hoped-for salvation within history. In her work *En La Lucha: A Hispanic Women's Liberation*, Isasi-Diáz names this historically embedded salvation the *proyecto historico*. To summarize, the *proyecto historico* is possible and built through the three aspects: 1) *libertad* (freedom), the self-actualization of individuals and communities, 2) *comunidad de fe* (faith community), a community meant to replace the systems of sin that dominate the current context, and 3) *justicia* (justice), the requirement of solidarity.[40] Regardless of race, class, gender, sexual orientation, or other aspects of our identity, we all have a responsibility to work towards the *proyecto historico* and participate. It is a radical, shared story of ultimate trust in our neighbor. This type of society, imagined as the *proyecto historico,* requires the participation of the whole community. The practice of living into the *proyecto historico* is a practice of both liberation and hope. Salvation cannot occur without liberation. For Isasi-Diáz, the resurrection and the *proyecto historico* are two aspects of one liberative process.[41] This process also includes the naming and denunciation of suffering and oppression. In order to announce the hoped-for future, the community must know, name, and reject the evil it opposes.[42] The practice of living into the *proyecto historico*, includes both the cross and resurrection, exemplifying the importance of their connection. The process of liberation requires both the denouncing of the cross and the announcement of the resurrection.

---

40. Isasi-Diáz, *En La Lucha,* 37.

41. Isasi-Diáz, *En La Lucha,* 52.

42. Isasi-Diáz, *En La Lucha,* 53.

At the center of the *proyecto historico* process is the role of community and community organizing. The community outlines and creates
ways for how we can be human to one another. Scholars call the community's role in interpreting God's hope for our future and the future of
the church the sense of the faithful: *sensus fidelium*. In this way, salvation
requires the work of the community for its realization and embodiment.
The hoped-for future is only attained through the work and organizing
of people in communities. For example, in her work in Ciudad Juárez,
Nancy Pineda-Madrid observed the role of community organizing in the
production of hope. She writes that the organizers and participants "have
tilted the community of Juárez and all of us toward the possibility of hope
and salvation."[43] Pineda-Madrid argues that we must "interpret salvation
socially" in order to heal our communities. The community's ability to
enact healing, embody hope, and further salvation is dependent on the
social aspects of salvation.

Practices of Resistance

Pineda-Madrid names the communal work for justice and salvation,
"practices of resistance." Similar to Sobrino's call to "take down the crucified ones" from the cross, also called "praxis of resurrection," "practices of
resistance" are ultimately ways for people to practice hope, resurrection,
and healing. What makes "practices of resistance" different from practices of "taking down the crucified ones" is that the victims are the agents
of hope in Pineda-Madrid's work. The victims take an active role in their
healing, rather than the passive role of "being taken down." The call to act
and practice resurrection with the oppressed of history, regardless of our
victimization, is important and part of our call to a discipleship of solidarity. But, in the case of "practices of resistance," survivors have agency,
ultimately subverting structures of power and violence. These practices
are a "public processing of pain," where survivors bring suffering and
injustice into the public eye, displaying a "firm commitment to act on
behalf of a better world."[44] "Practices of resistance" help to ensure that a
community shapes a practice of the resurrection in accordance with their
context, resulting in appropriate and meaningful practices of hope.

43. Pineda-Madrid, *Suffering and Salvation*, 152.
44. Pineda-Madrid, *Suffering and Salvation*, 117.

Through "Practices of resistance," survivors incorporate their story of suffering. Survivors root these practices within their contexts and point to how salvation in history might look. Pineda-Madrid asks: "What does it mean to take seriously the historical nature of salvation? . . . salvation in history will be worked out differently depending upon the given historical context, its time and place."[45] Salvation in Ciudad Juárez answers to the horrific reality of *feminicide*. Salvation and "practices of resistance" look a particular way in this community. For example, survivors, mourners, and protestors of the systematic killing of the city's young women created and enacted "practices of resistance," many of which are public acts: marches, public vigils, demonstrations, memorials, etc. Because the perpetrators of *feminicide* kill outside of the public eye, bringing the suffering to public attention is an important part of denouncing the evil of *feminicide*. Similarly, the Gospel of Mark does this by proclaiming that God has accepted the crucified, the rejected. The narrative vindication of the Suffering Innocent One subverts the public shaming of the cross. "Practices of resistance" act as a reversal of the evil they are resisting. Like the early Jesus community, many of the practices in Juárez also subvert common symbols, such as the cross, to question the systems that allow this evil to continue. In using the pink crosses of Juárez, protestors are posing the radical question of how is the cross changed when women are placed at the center? And because public officials blame these women for their fates, does the act of connecting the rejected and violated to the cross change their public image and persona? The radical nature of this practice, a community holding up the rejected victim as the example of a life cherished and accepted by God, mirrors the narrative effects of Mark's passion.

"Practices of resistance" not only provide agential and subversive language to think about resurrection, but also a sense that suffering remains after healing. The reality is that an understanding of salvation and healing that is contextual, also means that we do not experience healing or salvation once and for all, but rather live life in a middle space. The narrative promises us redemption, but does not deny our current context of suffering. Pineda-Madrid writes that "through the practices, participants negotiate the place in between despair and hope; in between the tragedy of crucifixion and the hope of vindication, the promise of a

---

45. Pineda-Madrid, *Suffering and Salvation*, 129.

resurrection."[46] The pink crosses of Juárez do not deny or hide the suffering of the cross or the victims of *feminicide*. In fact, by implementing the symbol of the cross in this way, participants and witnesses bring the "tragedy of crucifixion" to the fore. Rather than denying the reality of suffering, these "practices of resistance" hold a space in which we can name the violence, without it holding the power of silence over us. The passion narrative in Mark is similar in both its depiction of Jesus as suffering and abandoned and its rejection of a clean and tidy ending.

The Empty Tomb as a Sign and Place of Hope

Before turning to resurrection after domestic violence, I want to return to the Empty Tomb to develop a biblical vision of resurrection that highlights practices of hope, building upon and complicating Gebara's "fragile redemption" and Pineda-Madrid's "practices of resistance." Specifically, as we discussed above, the original ending of Mark's Gospel, gives us an early, female-focused, ambiguous, trauma-informed, account of the resurrection, written for a community on the edge of the apocalypse. Serene Jones, calls this ending an "unending," pointing out that unfinished qualities leave "room for the embodied experience of [survivors of trauma]."[47] These unending aspects of Mark's Empty Tomb speaks to the perpetual cycle of suffering and salvation we have explored above as "fragile redemption. My hope, in engaging this resurrection narrative absent of a resurrected Jesus, is to find a trauma-informed space for meaning making for survivors of domestic violence. The final line of Mark's original ending reads, "So they went out and fled from the tomb, for terror and amazement has seized them; and they said nothing to anyone, for they were afraid."[48] But before this final line, there is the account of the women at the Empty Tomb. Unlike Jones' interpretation, I argue the Empty Tomb tradition does not just give us silence and gesture towards embodiment in which to make meaning, but also gives us an example of "practices of resistance" in the actions of the women who came to the tomb to be present to each other and the crucified body of Jesus. I will examine these actions and moments for their ability to move us through abandonment

---

46. Pineda-Madrid, *Suffering and Salvation*, 150.

47. Jones, *Trauma and Grace*, 97.

48. Mark 16:8, NRSV.

and weariness, searching for how they embody hope, comfort and heal us.

The Empty Tomb narrative maintains a close relationship with the crucifixion. Many appearance accounts in the tradition preserve this connection as well, presenting the resurrected Jesus with crucifixion wounds. The Empty Tomb tradition does this by not fully resolving the suffering of witnessing the cross for the women. The women are left unsure and terrified of what has happened. They are told Jesus has gone ahead of them, but this requires that they work towards the future for the full realization of this vision —a message spoken to the women but intended for the audience. The women are left with overlapping cross and resurrection moments, mirroring Gebara's "fragile redemption" and the experiences of trauma survivors. The Empty Tomb leaves space for the suffering of crucifixion to remain within moments of resurrection, holding up and acknowledging the reality of suffering the women and the audience continued to experience. The Empty Tomb tradition is important for its ambiguity in regards to the resurrection because it does not symbolically reverse the suffering of the cross through the bodily appearance of Jesus, making it an important conversational partner for thinking about hope after trauma and suffering in the lives of survivors of domestic violence. The Empty Tomb narrative acknowledges the reality that life is a series of crosses and resurrections, leaving room for both these experiences. I argue that the Empty Tomb is a site of "fragile redemption"—or fragile *resurrection*—where the women disciples of Jesus perform "practices of resistance"—or hope.

Mark's ending leaves the resurrection open-ended and unfinished, presenting an image of *fragile resurrection*. It is a resurrection that does not completely dispel the fears and anxieties of suffering. The suffering of the crucifixion haunts the Empty Tomb. To this same end, the Markan Empty Tomb narrative can be read back into the crucifixion moment. The crucifixion is no longer devoid completely of hope. The author hints at a fragile resurrection in the crucifixion moment, because it is part of the larger narrative of vindication and acceptance. Similarly, in the Gospel of Mark, the same women who go to the Empty Tomb are also steadfast in their presence at the crucifixion six verses before, witnessing the cross from a distance (Mark 15:40). These women not only maintain a literary cohesiveness between the crucifixion and resurrection accounts, but they also embody both the hope and suffering present in both moments of the cross and resurrection as experienced by the early Jesus community.

Their choice to practice radical solidarity and stay with Jesus at the cross and the resurrection paradoxically embody both the suffering and pain of losing Jesus, their teacher, friend, son, and companion, as well as the hope that this is not the end.

The women in the Empty Tomb narrative choose to accompany Jesus through the crucifixion and at the tomb. While in Mark's narrative, they ultimately fail—an important point for Mark, who wants their audience to pick up where the male and female disciples fall short in their duty to true discipleship—we can re-imagine the women's practice of presence, regardless of how terrified they were, as a "practice of resistance." In the Empty Tomb narrative, the women, Mary Magdalene, Mary mother of James, and Salome, arrange to finish preparing Jesus' body for burial.[49] The Jewish burial practices of washing, anointing, and wrapping a body were most often performed before burial and at home.[50] But in the case of a criminal, the state would have barred Jesus' family from this tradition. Therefore, the narrative inclusion by Mark of the women not only accompanying the body in death, but also preparing to anoint the body, in an attempt to ritually correct the violation of crucifixion, can be read as a radical example of suffering discipleship and solidarity. After witnessing the horrific murder of someone so close to them, the women disciples of Jesus respond with practices of hope. Gebara imagines that "[w]omen stand around his cross as his friends, caring for his lifeless body so that life will not be further violated. This gesture is rich and symbolic because it leads to life. There are followers, men and women, who declare by their solidarity that unjust death does not have the last word."[51] In this way as well, the Empty Tomb is a site of hope. It is where the suffering and traumatized women disciples of Jesus gather to practice radical solidarity and loyalty with the crucified one. And Mark wants his audience to see that the Romans do not have the last word. Similar to Pineda-Madrid's "practices of resistance," the women gathered not only to mourn their loss, but to be present to the body and anoint it, searching for a way forward and refusing to give into their fear. Their presence to each other and intended presence to the body of Jesus, was a step forward.

The steps towards hope taken by Mark's depiction of the women disciples are met with a promise that God is trustworthy and an

49 "When the Sabbath was over, Mary Magdalene, and Mary the mother of James, and Salome bought spices, so that they might go and anoint him" (Mark 16:1, NRSV).

50. Brink and Green, *Commemorating the Dead*, 161–63.

51. Gebara, *Out of the Depths*, 115.

announcement of the hoped-for future. While more ambiguous on the state of the resurrected Jesus, the young man promises Jesus' location and presence to the women disciples and gives them a role to play in this promised future as well. The young man in the tomb tells the women that Jesus has gone ahead of them on the road. Jesus has not returned to heaven, but will be with them soon. This is a future oriented promise that Jesus has gone ahead of the women and the women must act by telling the other disciples and joining him. Schüssler Fiorenza points out that the Empty Tomb narrative focuses on a future oriented promise and call to be present with Jesus, rather than some of the later resurrection appearances that are more confessional in nature and function to give authority to male disciples.[52] This future oriented promise, that Jesus will be present on the road ahead of them, is concrete and practical and signals resurrection, healing, and hope. God has not forgotten them. The young man calls the women disciples and the audience to practice hope through radical solidarity with the crucified.

But Mark does not depict this. The women leave the tomb in silence and fear. Is this an ultimate rejection of that mission, that the author intended in order to move their audience to action? Or are there clues to the contrary that would have signalled to the Markan audience that the women do continue their practice of suffering discipleship and solidarity? Regardless, the effect on the audience is the same. The author calls them to live as true disciples, through radical suffering, solidarity, and loyalty to the crucified of history. And in doing this, even if it leads to death or rejection, God will not forget them.

Just as the author intended the narrative of the women at the Empty Tomb to help the audience make sense of their own practices of hope and healing, pushing them to move forward from their trauma, we can connect this fragile resurrection to the healing and salvation of women today. Survivors of violence today can see the choices and agency of the women at the tomb as an example of how to hold and work through trauma healing. This resurrection narrative is radical, not because of the singularity and conclusiveness of Jesus' resurrection, but exactly because the choices of the women at the tomb and Jesus' resurrection are deeply connected to the vindication and healing of the crucified throughout history. The women of the Empty Tomb practice presence and solidarity with the abandoned Jesus and in doing so, change their reality, creating a hope

52. Schüssler Fiorenza, *Jesus*, 123–26.

that proves that death and suffering were not final. Rather than practices
of optimism, these were practices of imagination that opened the future.
And the practices of radical, suffering discipleship and solidarity from
these women make the Empty Tomb a key conversation partner for con-
templating resurrection after trauma.

In light of this historical context, the nature of the narrative, and the
insights of fragile resurrection and practices of resistance, I put forward
a renewed account of Mark's Empty Tomb. In this renewed account, the
world is ending. The audience looks on as a small group of disciples gather at a distance to witness the death of their beloved teacher and friend.
This scene is jarringly similar to the experiences of war and oppression
of the past several years under Rome. A cross is at the center of the scene
and reawakens the fear of death and destruction many in the audience
have lived with recently. Most of the players who are left on stage are
the women disciples, signaling the abandonment and decimation of this
community.

Yet the women remain loyal. True disciples of solidarity. The audience understands deeply in their bones the importance of loyalty and
solidarity to their own survival. This scene, the women watching their
Beloved suffer and die, would echo the audience's own experiences and
continued nightmares. This community is on the edge and it seems all
that is left for them is to wait for their total annihilation. But many in the
audience won't die. And this narrative teaches them how to tell and reframe their story, remembering and denouncing their pain and suffering.
This narrative followed the familiar reframing of the Suffering Innocent
Ones and because of this the audience knows God will vindicate them
too. Their pain and suffering were not just theirs, but the pain and suffering of all the poor and oppressed.

The three women remain on stage, long after others have taken
the cross down and all the male actors have abandoned the body. The
women on stage spend the day and night in mourning, telling stories,
and sharing the long moments of silence. They then begin to gather their
oils and ointments for preparing the body of their dead loved one. The
audience knows this practice intuitively, but now see it anew, as a practice
of resistance. The women choose loyalty and radical solidarity, refusing
to give in to their context. But the audience wonders with the women
how they will access the tomb. The tomb of a criminal would certainly be
closed to mourners. But in the next scene, the women and the audience
discover the way has been cleared. And inside a young man, depicted in

white and with an angelic presence, announces that Jesus has been raised. Immediately the audience understands two things. First, that Jesus, as the Suffering Innocent One, has been accepted and vindicated by God. And second, they will ultimately share the fate of Jesus in the end.

As the four figures stand together on stage, in the tomb, the audience knows they are not alone. In that moment, there is hope, but it is a fragile resurrection. They are able to see their future selves moving forward, past the persecution and death of their current context. They see a future they can not fully comprehend. But it is fragile, like their lives under the powers and principalities of this world. The moment of hope passes and the trauma and exhaustion returns. At this point, all players exit and the audience is left with an empty tomb, and a call to suffering discipleship and solidarity in order that God will vindicate them as well.

Understanding Resurrection after the Empty Tomb: Healing from Domestic Violence

How do the experiences of healing after domestic violence reshape and push these concepts of hope and the narrative of the Empty Tomb developed above? With the purpose of extending these theological ideas of hope to the context of healing after domestic violence, I turn to the specific voices and experiences of survivors of domestic violence in the next chapter. Both concepts of "fragile redemption" and "practices of resistance" give us nuanced ways of engaging healing after suffering, but also highlight places for growth in our understanding of resurrection.

While "fragile redemption" creates an important space for healing after suffering, it ultimately obscures salvation's connection to the resurrection. Gebara does this intentionally to expand redemption beyond the singular cross and resurrection of Jesus. But in Gebara's disconnection of salvation from the cross and resurrection of Jesus, we lose access to a potentially radical narrative found in the stories of the early Jesus community. We lose something important in fully disconnecting the experiences of daily hope from the resurrection event of Jesus. I argue that in connecting the daily experiences of hope and healing of survivors of domestic violence more directly with the world of meaning of the Gospel of Mark, both events are re-imagined in their significance and relevance.

"Practices of resistance" described as "public processing of pain,"[53] provide us with public, communal practices of hope. By turning to the experiences of domestic violence survivors, a suffering within the private sphere, I will expand "practices of resistance" to include the more private, mundane, and obligatory practices of life. This is particularly poignant in an era of social isolation and distancing. As the pandemic reshapes and blocks our public spaces, there is a need for a deep re-imagining of our human natures' connection to God and the work of salvation at a private and familial level. And in a particular context where the most intimate relationship has been violated, practices of hope after domestic violence must heal the private sphere. To investigate these questions further in the next chapter, I turn to the narratives, voices, and practices of domestic violence survivors of House of Peace. House of Peace is a Chicago-based domestic violence shelter run by the Catholic Church in Waukegan, a northern suburb of Chicago. Started in 2011, House of Peace set out to address the issue of domestic violence in their community. As we will more fully explore in the next chapter, the survivors at House of Peace, experience their restoration and healing particularly in the moments of community around the kitchen table. Practices of hope after domestic violence need to restore our innate connection with God through the self and each other in the private moments of our lives. We find restoration in the moments we take for ourselves and each other: early morning quiet cups of coffee, watching our children play, taking time to be in nature, consciously creating safe and comfortable spaces for ourselves, telling our stories.

The women of House of Peace narrate their experiences of trauma and healing within the framing tale of Jesus' crucifixion and resurrection. What transpires is a dialogue between the gospel narratives and these women's experiences of healing after domestic violence, resulting in the metanoia and reshaping of both tradition and practice. In the next chapter, I will interrogate the depiction of resurrection we find in the Markan Empty Tomb and the narrations of domestic violence survivors, in order to renew and transform both stories. In doing this, I hope to provide new insight into the Markan tradition of the Empty Tomb. The stories and interviews of the survivors at House of Peace give us a new way to read and understand the Empty Tomb account, as well as resurrection in the midst of trauma.

---

53. Pineda-Madrid, *Suffering and Salvation*, 117.

In my search for hope after domestic violence, a deeper exploration of the crucifixion and resurrection as developed by feminist liberation theologians was necessary. Feminist liberation theologians, Gebara and Pineda-Madrid, turn to the multiple moments of crucifixion and resurrection as experienced by women in their suffering and healing. Women as "crucified people" become "risen beings" through "practices of resistance" in moments of "fragile redemption," as exemplified by the women disciples in Mark's Empty Tomb narrative. The resurrection narrative found in the Empty Tomb ultimately challenges the extrinsic, singular view of Jesus' resurrection, revealing that our relationships with others mediate a resurrection that repeats throughout our lives and history. Resurrection hope is not something we achieve once and for all; rather we must practice hope within every new contextual experience of suffering and crucifixion.

In my search for practices of hope after domestic violence, the next chapter will continue to develop the concepts of hope and the Empty Tomb narrative I have explored above. Building off Gebara's "fragile redemption," the hope practiced at the Empty Tomb was more clearly connected to the resurrection of Jesus. The fragile *resurrection* moment of the Empty Tomb maintains a strong connection of salvation and healing to the experiences of the cross and resurrection of Jesus. The Empty Tomb's fragile resurrection more clearly bonds everyday hope with the singular event of Jesus' resurrection. Fragile resurrection is a moment in which we experience healing in the wake of suffering, but it is not once and for all, nor guaranteed. The fragility of these moments does not undermine the power of resurrection, but rather highlights that resurrection is always contextual.

The term fragile *resurrection* extends Gebara's "fragile redemption" beyond the daily lived experience of suffering and healing of individuals. Crucifixion and resurrection narratives play a large role in shaping our understanding of salvation for good and for bad. The crucifixion and resurrection of Jesus are part of the theological imaginations of many survivors of domestic violence, and rather than focusing exclusively on their own experiences of hope and healing, re-imagining Jesus' resurrection can help them to connect their experiences together as a community and to a larger narrative frame about hope and healing. Essentially, fragile resurrection connects the daily crosses and resurrections of women back to the larger theological and communal traditions of salvation represented in the resurrection of Jesus. Fragile resurrection moments give us insight and revelation into the deeper truth and meaning behind Jesus resurrection, in the same way the gospel accounts of Jesus' resurrection can illuminate the daily experiences of healing.

The Empty Tomb narrative also expands Pineda-Madrid's "practices of resistance." The women disciples embody hope and enact salvation in their presence at the Empty Tomb through hope practices. Like Pineda-Madrid's "practices of resistance," hope after domestic violence identifies the evil that has caused moments of crucifixion, while also working to subvert that same evil through symbols and acts of hope. Practices of hope after domestic violence focus on embodying hope in the present time, in the midst of uncertainty, when future promises of a more radical and final salvation have yet to be fully realized. Pushing "practices of resistance" further, hope after domestic violence—an event in which survivors experience disconnection from themselves, others, and God—must mediate the salvation of Jesus' resurrection in daily life and not just in moments of resistance or public protest. The sacramental nature of our daily lives allows for survivors to practice hope and enact salvation in small and seemingly inconsequential moments of healing after domestic violence. In the next chapter, we will re-imagine and challenge the Markan Gospel narrative of the Empty Tomb in light of the voices and narratives of survivors of domestic violence. Specifically, we turn to the former residents of House of Peace, a Chicago-based domestic violence shelter, and their stories of trauma, healing, and hope.

4

House of Peace

A Case Study of Resurrection after Domestic Violence

SCHOLARS DEBATE THE ORIGINAL narrative purpose of the Empty Tomb ending in Mark. Whether this part of the narrative was a reenactment of funeral rituals or a narrative choice by the author to further connect Jesus to the suffering Innocent One, the Empty Tomb speaks to an audience on the edge of the world. In her sixth chapter of *Trauma and Grace: Theology in a Ruptured World*, "Unending Cross," Serene Jones explores the Empty Tomb narrative for its ability to act as a modern script for performance, that provides silence and an embodied directive for survivors of trauma. Jones argues that the "unending" of the Empty Tomb leaves the audience with a space for contemplation and unanswered questions. In this chapter, I would like to expand Jones' conclusion about the Empty Tomb. In dialogue with the women of House of Peace, the Empty Tomb becomes prescriptive, showing us an example of how to practice and embody hope after trauma. The residents of House of Peace become the women disciples who gather at the Empty Tomb, practicing hope through presence to each other. The current embodiment of hope in the women of House of Peace actually sheds light on the deeper meaning and material formation of the Empty Tomb narrative we find in Mark.

The resurrection narrative echoes throughout history, playing itself out again and again. Today, in the voices of the women at House of Peace, we see another iteration. *The violence was increasing with my husband until the time came when the children and I felt more secure when he was not in the house.* That was the biggest motivating factor for her—safety. It wasn't for lack of love, or wanting to change her life. It was the fear that if he decided to, he could take everything away.

I entered House of Peace very fearful, because someone else always decided for me; I feared that something would happen to my children and me. I felt responsible for what would happen to them, because I was the one who took them out of the house. Their home. How terrifying to leave everything behind and move to live in a house with strangers? She had already started over once before, when she had left Mexico for Chicago. Why did this happen again? *The hardest time was the first few weeks when I arrived* at House of Peace. *I have two children and that was the hardest thing for me, the first three weeks that they didn't see* their father *and I didn't know how to tell them or to explain the situation that we were living in. Those were for me the most complicated and difficult days.* At least at home she had known the warning signs of when things were going to get bad. She knew how to protect her children from his abuse. Who were these other people at the shelter? All unknown factors. How could they expect her to trust them?

At the first sign that this was the wrong choice for her children, she would leave. *If my children are happy I am happy if my children are well I am well. They are my motor, for them I keep going. I get up and I move forward, and I know that God doesn't leave me alone. That's why he gave me these two little motors because he knows that without them I fall apart. He put them there so that I could go on, and so I will.* She would go on. In fact, their transformation at House of Peace became one of the first signs that leaving her husband had been right for her and them.

As time passed in the shelter, it began to feel like a home. *They trust that* House of Peace *is a place where they can find God. It's a place where they trust in an encounter with God. Part of that is just because of the style of relating very intimately, very family-like, partly it is the fact that we encourage this to be a community of support, we eat together, we struggle together, we pray together, they share their burden with one another.* The strangers became trustworthy. They became family. She practiced creating and sustaining the family life her abusive partner and society had denied her for so long. *It happens in the kitchen and the halls. You see these women healing each other, and sometimes their children.* Time, space, food, prayer, all worked their incomprehensible magic to create this home.

Most importantly, they shared their stories. *The other moms during my stay in the house were also important because we shared the same experiences. We all lived together and little by little we were sharing our experiences of violence and of trauma that we all had . . . We came from the same situation, and we all encouraged each other.* Through their shared experiences a foundation was set. Their shared trauma became a touchstone. *Sometimes we think that we won't find the light that we are looking for. That nobody will get you out of that dark place. You think that no one will give you a hand, but nevertheless there are people who do it without asking for anything in return.* The months at the shelter passed quickly, she and her family began to flourish. A new vision of the future became opened to them—a future of a radically loving home.

She now understands her own self-worth and the possibilities her life has. *What gives me hope is that we are all here for a purpose. It made me see that God made us so perfect, and He also gives us so many dreams. And we can make those dreams happen. If we work on them we can achieve them.* The trauma and suffering of her life before remain with her, a specter, a reminder, but it has been remembered into meaning. The abuse carried no meaning in and of itself, but she has created meaning out of it. She has gathered her strength and re-narrates her pain. *They acknowledge their pain and their woundedness. When they go into it they are really starting to move, create movement in the spirit, I feel. By just acknowledging is a way of validating themselves by visiting the pain. And sometimes it's pain that has been there a long time.* She leaves the shelter, forever marked by her experiences of suffering and healing, moving into a future that she can only begin to imagine.

"We Came from the Same Situation": Remembering Trauma Together

"There were also women looking on from a distance; among them were Mary Magdalene, and Mary the mother of James the younger and of Joses, and Salome. These used to follow him and provided for him when he was in Galilee; and there were many other women who had come up with him to Jerusalem."

MARK 15:40–41

"The other moms during my stay in the house were also important because we shared the same experiences. We all lived together and little by little we were sharing our experiences of violence and of trauma that we all had . . .

We came from the same situation, and we all encouraged each other . . .
Sometimes we think that we won't find the light that we are looking for. That
nobody will get you out of that dark place. You think that no one will give
you a hand, but nevertheless there are people who do it without asking for
anything in return and for me that is very important."

MARTINA, FORMER RESIDENT OF HOUSE OF PEACE

Just before the narrative of the Empty Tomb, in Mark's crucifixion account, the author notes that a group of women witness Jesus' execution.
In contrast to the male disciples, who, at this point in the narrative, have
all denied their connection to Jesus or fled, this group of women disciples choose to remain with Jesus during his final hours on the cross.
The author names three women in the group (Mary Magdalene, Mary the
mother of James the younger and of Joses, and Salome), possibly signaling their significance to Mark's audience and the early Christian community. These same three also stay through the burial and, later, come to the
Empty Tomb. The role and importance of staying with each other, both
hearing and telling stories, came up throughout my conversations with
the women of House of Peace. The residents create a strong community
of witnesses in the aftermath of their own experiences of suffering and
the women often cited this role as a source of healing. The significance
of choosing to listen to each other's pain in the lives of the women at
House of Peace, calls us to look more closely at the women's role at the
crucifixion in Mark's gospel. Storytelling, witnessing, and naming suffering takes on a crucial role for the healing and community building of
both the women of House of Peace and the women of the early Christian
community.

At House of Peace, both sharing and listening to stories are a daily
part of life. From the jocular banter the women exchange in quick Spanish while cooking, to the hushed reflections over late-night cups of coffee
after work while the children sleep, the women become each other's closest confidants. And eventually many of them begin to open up about the
experiences of violence and abuse that ultimately brought them and their
children to the shelter. The design of the "Resurrection Stories" project
reflects this need for survivors to share and be heard. There is a need
in our communities to hear these narratives as well, re-imagining the
cross and resurrection in fleshed out and non-sterile ways. The project
not only encourages the women to narrate their experiences, but many

of the testimonies highlight the healing role that connecting over similar experiences played for the residents. One narrative, displayed next to a colorful cross painted brightly to depict a nature scene of a tree next to water with the word "Esperanza" (hope) and two doves across the center, reads, "I have learned to share my story with others and to listen to their stories too. We all share similar previous experiences . . . Many of us have felt lonely and we have even felt despair. We all feel blessed now by sharing our lives with each other."[1] For survivors of trauma, learning to put one's experience of trauma into words is an important part of the healing process, but more significantly, for the survivors at House of Peace, sharing these stories creates a strong foundation for the community as a whole.

It stands to reason, the narrative of the women at the cross in Mark could have had a similar effect on the early Christian community as the stories shared between survivors at House of Peace. We can re-imagine the narrative Mark creates, where the women choose to be at the cross and present to this persecution, mirrors the experience of many of the audience members who lived under Roman oppression, and continued towards hope. In light of the power that narratives of shared traumatic experience have to heal a community, the women at the cross in Mark's gospel serve a similar touchpoint for the audience. Like the women at House of Peace, survivors of trauma in the audience of Mark's gospel can identify with the women, creating a foundational experience that helps to ground and strengthen the early community of Jesus-followers through a shared traumatic event.

For the survivors at House of Peace, an important part of narrating their experiences of abuse is naming and denouncing their suffering. From similar abuse tactics, to feelings of isolation and despair, many of the women described their lives within their abusive relationship in shared themes and language, echoing each other. The survivors I spoke with often associated feelings of loneliness, frustration, fear, and despair with their time before the shelter, when they were in the midst of abuse. Many of the women wrote narratives that reflected on their experiences of abuse, identifying and naming the evil within their experience. One "Resurrection Story" displayed alongside a vivid blue cross with a dove and rays of light shining onto a newly fruiting grapevine. This story described a life of abuse. "My life has been confusing, complicated and very

---

1. House of Peace, "My Cross: HOPE."

stressed out" the survivor reflects. "Living each day with a person that I was afraid of due to his aggressive attitude made me an ill-humored, defensive person. I worried much about our lives and started to feel physically weak."[2] The stress and anxiety produced by this survivor's circumstance resulted in the loss of her bodily-health. Living in a constant state of fear or anxiety produces detrimental health effects. Another testimony recounts feelings of helplessness, reading "I felt trapped and with no escape, wondering how I could change my life and the lives of my daughters. I was very worried about how I would provide food for them since I was economically dependent. I was always asking God to help me."[3] This description not only echoes other testimonies of domestic violence, but also Jesus' crucifixion itself. She cries out to God for help, in a way that connects her voice to Jesus' cries to God while on the cross. The experiences of suffering, isolation, and helplessness are uncannily cruciform in their retelling, mirroring the Markan depiction of Jesus' abandonment on the cross. The experiences of abuse recounted in these narratives underscore the deep connection many of these survivors feel with the suffering of Christ in the passion narratives.

As the women narrate their experiences of suffering and domestic violence as cross-like, they find a framing story that helps them to make sense of their experiences through narrative and imagination. These personal moments of crucifixion and resurrection do not justify the domestic violence, but rather the narrative of the Suffering Innocent One becomes a scaffold upon which the women can place their own stories of suffering, in the same way that Mark's author used this narrative to make sense of Jesus' death. This framing narrative brings order to the chaos of a traumatic life experience. By naming their suffering as connected to Jesus' death, these survivors are able to denounce their experiences of suffering to each other and the larger community in the public exhibit of the "Resurrection Stories." The survivors at House of Peace make sense and name their experience of suffering by connecting it to a larger epidemic of abuse and oppression of women, choosing to connect their individual experiences of pain and loss to a larger historical reality of suffering, represented in the cross. Through this work of narrative and imagination, the women connect themselves to each other, the women

---

2. House of Peace, "Finding Spiritual Strength."

3. House of Peace, "My Cross: My Strength."

who choose to stay with Jesus through his crucifixion, and the larger Christian community.

"For Them I Keep Going": Mary and Motherhood

"The surrounding rosary represents the companionship of the Virgin Mary, who was always present in the life of Jesus. She was with him up to his last days, embracing him on the cross. This is just like the love of God and is reflected in Jesus and his mother."

MY CROSS: THE LOVE OF GOD REFLECTED IN JESUS AND THE VIRGIN MARY, HOUSE OF PEACE RESURRECTION STORY

"The hardest time was the first few weeks when I arrived [at House of Peace]. . . I have two children and that was the hardest thing for me, the first three weeks that they didn't see [their father] and I didn't know how to tell them or to explain the situation that we were living in. Those were for me the most complicated and difficult days . . . If my children are happy I am happy if my children are well I am well. They are my motor, for them I keep going. I get up and I move forward, and I know that God doesn't leave me alone. That's why he gave me these two little motors because he knows that without them I fall apart. He put them there so that I could go on, and so I will."

MARIANA, FORMER RESIDENT OF HOUSE OF PEACE

Mary, the mother of Jesus, is both a comforting and relatable figure for many of the women at House of Peace. Mary has a strong presence in the practices of Latino/a forms of Catholicism and theologians and practitioners often portray her as a model for motherhood. For these reasons, the women at House of Peace see Mary as a companion in their healing journey. The children (newborns-18 years old) often outnumber the adult residents significantly and for the women to meet the needs of all the children staying at the house, daily activities often focus around them, including tutoring, scheduled activities, school bus pick-ups and drop-offs, and making sure everyone is fed. During my visits at House of Peace, the women had decorated the house with images and figures of Mary, especially in the form of Our Lady of Guadalupe. In my discussion with the residents, they often named Mary as both an intercessor and an example of motherhood.

While Mark's Gospel erases Mary, the mother of Jesus, her role in other gospels, especially John's Gospel, is significant. Some scholars argue Mark's author obscures Mary's presence by using different names to identify her, while others believe there may have been multiple Mary's related to Jesus in some way. While Mary's role in Mark's gospel is less than other gospels and debated among scholars, Mary is a significant figure for the women at House of Peace. In both interviews and "Resurrection Stories," the women referenced Mary's choice to stay with her son through the crucifixion, reflecting the radical suffering discipleship and solidarity found in Mark's Gospel. Many of the residents reflected on Mary's own experiences of trauma and suffering at the foot of the cross during Jesus' death, a scene that is only present in the Gospel of John. Her unending presence, love, and experience of suffering makes her a relatable and comforting figure, if not a problematic idealization of passivity in suffering. Mary also functions as a reminder of the paradoxical nature of motherhood as something that is powerful, as well as fragile—a gift, as well as a burden. While full of complexities and pitfalls, motherhood was ultimately described as both a motivator for transformation and a source of unending love for many of the women at House of Peace. And this insight deepens the original narrative to include an important missing piece to the crucifixion and resurrection narrative we find in Mark's gospel.

In Latina theology, the figure of Mary plays a central role as an exemplar for women and a major figure around which imagination and re-contextualization center. Theologians, Ivone Gebara and María Clara Bingemer, collect and construct a liberation mariology in their work *Mary: Mother of God, Mother of the Poor*, which focuses on the creative tradition of Mary within Latin America and her role as a figure of hope.[4] Gebara and Bingemer do not rehash old-fashioned notions of the ideal woman and mother through the symbol of Mary, but rather re-read Mary in light of modern understandings of sex, gender, and historical consciousness. In the same way we must re-imagine the cross or resurrection in light of our contexts, "the life of Mary of Nazareth is always taking place anew."[5] With this renewal in mind, I would argue that Mary shares

---

4. Gebara and Bingemer, *Mary: Mother of God*, xii.

5. Gebara and Bingemer, *Mary: Mother of God*, 18.

much of her identity and experience with the women at House of Peace. She is a refugee mother, who experiences doubt, struggle, and suffering. And yet, while not a tent pole for the Markan community and narrative, Mary becomes a major figure for women and mothers the world over (especially in Catholicism).

We can find a more complex understanding of Mary and mother-hood in the "Resurrection Stories" of House of Peace. These portrayals of Mary are in stark contrast to the common portrayals we find in more patriarchal texts, art, and icons. Figures such as the "Virgin Mary," the "humble handmaid," and the "empty vessel" often overemphasize pas-sivity as the central characteristic of women. Complicating the role and figure of Mary in Christianity, Elizabeth Schüssler Fiorenza argues that the cult of Mary has long been used to systematically control and op-press women. The cult of Mary has historically devalued women in three ways: 1) an overemphasis on virginity, 2) an equation of womanhood with motherhood, and 3) overstressing obedience, humility, passivity, and submission.[6] Since passivity can be a particularly dangerous charac-teristic to idealize in situations of abuse, it makes sense that the women of House of Peace read Mary in a different light.

House of Peace's relationship with Mary becomes even richer when we consider the figure of Our Lady of Guadalupe, who is not only con-nected to the patriarchy of the Church but also colonialism. Colonialism acts as a current and historical force, shaping the culture and lives of the Hispanic community at House of Peace. When the community identi-fies with a colonial figure such as Our Lady of Guadalupe, there may be a number of negative and unknown consequences. And yet, Mary has been empowering for Latina feminists, who have re-imagined her as an important figure in both her humanity and her embodiment of the hu-man potential for divine creativity.[7] Mary's humanness embodies God's promise, making her a central figure of embodied hope for the women of House of Peace, but a hope that is not without doubt, contradiction, and suffering.

One "Resurrection Story," painted with the images of a heart and rosary, addresses Mary's presence in the Gospel of John at the crucifixion as a comforting figure. The narrative reads, "The surrounding rosary rep-resents the companionship of the Virgin Mary, who was always present

6. Schüssler Fiorenza, *Jesus*, 165.

7. Gebara and Bingemer, *Mary: Mother of God*, 64.

in the life of Jesus. She was with him up to his last days, embracing him on the cross. This is just like the love of God and is reflected in Jesus and his mother."[8] For this survivor, the figure of Mary at the crucifixion is the embodied presence of God and the love of a Mother for her child is something holy, powerful, and sustaining. For many of the women of House of Peace, Mary is a powerhouse of strength, compassion, love, and the embodiment of the fierceness of motherhood. The House of Peace "Resurrection Stories" give us insight into the presence and strength of Mary in new and intertextual ways that expands beyond Mark's Gospel and other contemporary Marian devotion found today, which often use the image of Mary and/or Guadalupe to keep women submissive and obedient.

For many of the survivors at House of Peace, their role as a mother and their relationships to their children is an important source of unconditional love and affection. It was also an important motivating factor for many of the women in acting towards healthier and more stable lives. Several of the women noted that during their stay at the house they became closer with their children and with the children of the other women. Many of the children became more demonstrative with their affection towards their mothers during their stay at the shelter. This love and affection plays a large role in creating the safe space many of the women find at House of Peace. In the same "Resurrection Story" that depicted the heart and rosary, the survivor describes her admission into the house and how the other women and the children helped her to transition into thinking of the shelter as a home. She writes, "I learn from each of the families, day by day. The tender love of the children, the hope and patience of the Moms, the smiles, and so much more."[9] For many of the women, coming to House of Peace allows them to re-establish healthy relationships with their children, relationships that may have been severely lacking within the abusive households the families left. The safe space, removed from physical and emotional threat, allows both the women and their children to reconnect after their experiences of violence and uncertainty.

Women often cite shared children as a factor in staying with an abusive partner. Mothers fear they will not get custody, will not be able to provide food and shelter, or do not want to hinder their children's access

8. House of Peace, "My Cross: The Love of God Reflected in Jesus and the Virgin Mary."

9. House of Peace, "My Cross: The Love of God Reflected in Jesus and the Virgin Mary."

to their fathers. One "Resurrection Story" expresses this common fear, reading "I felt trapped and with no escape, wondering how I could change my life and the lives of my daughters. I was very worried about how I would provide food for them since I was economically dependent."[10] This survivor's feelings of responsibility for her children's safety and happiness worked to compound her feelings of powerlessness. The fear of the unknown future was ultimately not enough to keep this woman from choosing to leave her abusive partner in order to protect her children.

Often portrayed and experienced as a physical and emotional burden, motherhood for many of the women at House of Peace becomes a source of strength. For many of the survivors, their children's safety and futures were motivating factors for them to leave their abusive relationship in the first place. In our discussion around her decision to come to House of Peace, one survivor, Martina, focused on the safety of her family. "It was very difficult at that time because I was lost. I didn't know what to do. But I also knew that by making the decision of coming here, it would be a good thing for me and my children. And above all to be safe. That's what made me make the decision to come here."[11] Another survivor being interviewed, Abril, put it very simply. When I asked her why her children motivated her she responded, "Because my children are my reason to live and for them I try to do things right."[12] In a third interview, Mariana described her children as her "motors," her sources of energy. Smiling, Mariana said "They are my motor, for them I keep going. I get up and I move forward, and I know that God doesn't leave me alone. That's why he gave me these two little motors because he knows that without them I fall apart. He put them there so that I could go on, and so I will."[13] In some ways, many of the children were more resilient in the transition into House of Peace, acting as sources of love and energy for their mothers. Significantly here, Mariana attributes the comfort, motivation, and presence of her children to God, who "doesn't leave [her] alone."[14]

In my discussions with the director of the house, Aida, she reflected on a similar point, describing the children as angelic interpreters, "objects

10. House of Peace, "My Cross: My Strength."

11. Martina, interviewed by Ashley Theuring.

12. Abril, interviewed by Ashley Theuring.

13. Mariana, interviewed by Ashley Theuring.

14. Mariana, interviewed by Ashley Theuring.

of transformation" for their mothers. I had asked her about her own sources of hope working in this field. She responded immediately that often the children in the house were what gave her the most hope. She explained to me, "Many of these kids are true angels for these moms. These kids are really objects of transformation themselves almost, because they are able to witness and many times they are the facilitators of moms finally letting go of the toxicity or the co-dependence, the fear of moving on." Here, Aida echoes Martina and Mariana who above cited their children as the motivating factors for ultimately leaving their abusive household. The children act as angelic interpreters, helping to point their mothers towards safety and healing. Aida continued, concluding that "[the children] inspire their moms. They give them a reason to look at themselves differently. So the children give me a lot of hope."[15] As we see in the stories of the residents, the dependency of their children caused them anxiety in leaving their relationship, but the children were also the impetus for the women to seek safety. In the best of circumstances, children make us want to be our best selves.

The "Resurrection Stories" and the survivors of House of Peace reveal the paradoxical natures of both motherhood and hope. In one way, many of the women experience the strength, power, and holiness of mothering, which we often miss in our contemporary portrayals of Mary and motherhood in general. A strength, power, and holiness that the women of House of Peace imagine in Mary throughout Jesus' life, death, and resurrection. Ideally, motherhood becomes a practice of hope into the future, a hope that is embodied by a child who will live into the future beyond their parents. In another way, the reality of motherhood can become an added pressure and barrier for women seeking safety from their abusive partners. Sexual assault or abusive relationships can force women into motherhood. Motherhood, especially represented in "the Virgin Mary," becomes an impossible standard, adding to the oppression and controllability of women in our society. The historical Mary may have felt a similar burden in her motherhood. Being a young, single, mother and refugee is a description that fits Mary as well as many of the House of Peace residents.

In the narratives and interviews of the survivors at House of Peace, the women extend the presence of Mary at the cross, found in the Gospel of John, to the tomb. Mary becomes a testament to the paradoxical

---

15. Aida Segura, interviewed by Ashley Theuring.

blessing and curse of being a mother. Mary's love for Jesus reveals not only the depths of human love, which accompaniment and respect help to ground, but also the suffering that we become vulnerable to in these types of deep interdependent relationships. When mothers imagine Mary, the mother of Jesus, as present to her son's death and burial preparations, as the women of the House of Peace do, the maternal relationship becomes a possible site for hope. While this source of hope is not always culti-vated, in the case of abusive or unhealthy mother-children relationships, mothering as a hope practice can reach great depths. The narratives and interviews of the women at House of Peace reinvent the Empty Tomb narrative and concepts of hope, placing Mary into the story, to reveal the paradoxical and tenuous nature of hope and hope practices.

"Someone Else Always Decided for Me": Subverting Duty through Practices of Love and Obligation

"When the sabbath was over, Mary Magdalene, and Mary the mother of James, and Salome bought spices, so that they might go and anoint him. And very early on the first day of the week, when the sun had risen, they went to the tomb."

MARK 16:1–2

"The violence was increasing with [my husband] until the time came when the children and I felt more secure when he was not in the house . . . I entered House of Peace very fearful, because someone else always decided for me; I feared that something would happen to my children and me. I felt responsible for what would happen to them, because I was the one who took them out of the house."

GLORIA, FORMER RESIDENT OF HOUSE OF PEACE

Mark's resurrection account begins with three women, Mary Magdalene, Mary the mother of James, and Salome, making their way back to the tomb of Jesus in order to finish the funeral rites that the Sabbath had interrupted.[16] As we saw in the previous chapter, there are several ways to understand this passage, depending on how the audience is to interpret

16. Marcus, *Mark 8–16*, 1082.

the purpose and intent of the women going to the tomb. Jewish burial customs at the time highlight the importance and obligation of preparing a body for burial with spices and oils as a way of expressing familial duty, as well as, love and respect.[17] For a number of reasons, historically, caring for the dead is a skill and art that is often practiced by women in a society. It is also a ritual and practice that can shape a culture at a fundamental level, embodying familial responsibilities, religious beliefs, and cosmological understandings. Caring for the dead is a paradoxical practice that bestows power and stigmatization on those who tradition obligates to perform it. The actions of the women going to Jesus' tomb signal both the obligations put on women to care for the dead and the power women hold in this ritual's practice. Caring for the dead, especially in the case of Jesus, who died as a criminal, can become a radical practice, providing tender, loving protection against the violations of execution. These actions, whether performed because of cultural pressures, love, or a mix of both, were not going to literally "undo" Jesus' death, but rather they were a way of symbolically healing and recovering Jesus from his violent and brutal death. Early Jesus followers may have constructed these scenes of women practicing ritual anointing, such as the Markan Empty Tomb, as a way of re-imagining the fate of Jesus.

A similar paradoxical practice is found in the actions of the survivors at House of Peace. The women take on the bulk of the child care duties in the aftermath of domestic violence. While society celebrates women, like those at House of Peace, for taking steps to protect themselves and their children, a little discussed result of this is that the women become single parents, taking on the full brunt of raising their children. In both my interviews with the survivors and the "Resurrection Stories," the importance and weight of this new role as a single mother or co-parent became a central theme. Like the paradox of motherhood itself, becoming a single-parent in the wake of domestic violence is both empowering and a burden. While the narrative of the Empty Tomb in Mark hints at the importance of the anointing ritual, the stories and experiences of becoming a single or co-parent from the survivors at House of Peace help to more fully enflesh and complicate the nature of such hope practices. For the women at House of Peace, the practice of childcare is both one of love and obligation and we can read a similar practice at the heart of Mark's Empty Tomb.

17. Brink and Green, *Commemorating the Dead*, 163.

Domestic violence disrupts the ability of families to provide safe, secure, and healthy homes for children. Often, even when the abusive partner does not target the children in the home, the children are still exposed and deeply affected by the abusive behaviors perpetrated towards their parent, resulting in emotional, psychological, and behavioral issues throughout their life. For children in abusive homes, a major protective factor against these effects is the strong and healthy attachment to an adult, most often the mother.[18] House of Peace works to cultivate healthy mother-child relationships, providing time, counseling, and a safe space for children and their mothers to begin cultivating secure attachments.

For many of the mothers, rebuilding their relationships with their children begins with strengthening their own sense of self and security in ways that were not possible from within an abusive relationship. One survivor wrote in her "Resurrection Story," which she displayed next to a cross painted with roses and a butterfly, that her time at the House of Peace helped her to set and reach a number of goals from paying rent to becoming a citizen.[19] For survivors of abuse, establishing this level of independence is a key part of the healing process. Abusive relationships work to strip individuals of their independence, often working to make survivors fully reliant on their abusers. A level of independence goes hand in hand with strengthening one's self-identity, and the ability to care for others and discern the trustworthiness of other relationships. In several of the "Resurrections Stories," the women write about their transformation into more confident and self-reliant people during their stay at House of Peace. One story recounts a survivor starting her own business, while another talks about the importance of being able to "pick yourself back up" after setbacks. These stories display a sense of grit and determination that develops during these survivors' healing processes. One former resident, Martina, a mother of two, expressed a similar sentiment in her interview. I asked her if she had noticed a change in herself during her time at the shelter and she expressed that she was better at responding to her children's needs. She reflected, "But in comparison to how I am now, I'm a more secure person, . . . a person whose children are the most important thing, they're the most important thing I have, and for them I want to have a better life, and be a better mom . . . I can't

18. Holt et al., "The Impact of Exposure."
19. House of Peace, "My Cross: Transformation."

compare with the woman I was before."[20] As the mothers become more self-secure they are able to provide and care for their children, cultivating the healthy and secure attachments necessary for the children's own healing processes.

The development of these healthy relationships works to help mitigate the psychological and emotional effects of the abuse for these children. Unfortunately, the burden of alleviating the effects of the abuse falls to the healthy partner, rather than the abuser. Several of the women told me in their interviews that they noticed a change in their children during their stay at the shelter. One survivor, Gabrielle, commented on the general change she saw in her children, saying that her children acted less stressed while at House of Peace. Martina, on the other hand, noted an even more dramatic transformation took place for her teenage daughter. For Martina's daughter her time at the house spanned not only her transition from an abusive household to a more secure and safe living situation, but also her experience of puberty. Martina described her daughter as someone who had been shy and reserved, but who now was contributing to the teen's support group and was much more involved in the shelter life. House of Peace helped create a framework for Martina to help her daughter through these difficult transitions.

While House of Peace works to support these mothers in their transition to becoming single parents (or co-parents depending on the particular situation), this does not change the fact that for many of these women being a single-mother was not what they had hoped for themselves. Motherhood is not always a choice. Returning to the figure of Mary, Schüssler Fiorenza calls the historical Mary a "dangerous memory," pointing out Mary's life was far from an ideal vision of motherhood. Mary, who was probably not much older than thirteen, was unmarried, pregnant, and living in an occupied country.[21] Echoing this reality, the mothers of House of Peace are struggling for survival. We cannot re-inscribe an idealized version of motherhood onto the women at House of Peace, and it is important to acknowledge that domestic violence has scarred their experiences of motherhood and roles as mothers. Like the "dangerous memory" of the historical Mariam above, there may be a compulsory and survivalist aspect to the childcare and mothering duties for the women at House of Peace.

20. Martina, interviewed by Ashley Theuring.

21. Schüssler Fiorenza, *Jesus*, 187.

But the obligatory nature of these practices does not inhibit them from having the possibility of producing hope and healing. The everyday practices of mothering and caring for children that take place at House of Peace seem mundane enough on their surface, but after the experience of domestic violence, for many of these families the safety of a healthy and secure household can be a radical experience. A survivor, who creates and practices a healthy family life, can even help to mitigate the psychological effects of the abuse on her children. Through loving and tender practices of parenting, the women are able to reclaim their roles as mothers and begin a healing process for their families. While these practices are compulsory, the women of House of Peace are able to take back and transform their family narratives through the ritualized (and radical) acts of caring for their own and each other's children.

In light of the paradoxical nature of mothering exemplified in the survivors of House of Peace, we can re-read the anointing practice of the women disciples at the tomb of Jesus. The women, who planned to prepare Jesus' body, may have felt obligation in preparing the body of Jesus. But they may also have felt it as healing for themselves and each other. As female leaders in their community, these women would have performed this act of preparing a body before. This familiar practice could help make sense of their experience over the past couple days. It could have helped these women to "make sense" of their extraordinary experience. By caring for and preparing the body of Jesus, as they would have if he had died of natural causes, the traumatic persecution and violence of the past days would have been set into a familiar narrative of death and mourning. Both of these practices, caring for children and preparing Jesus' body for burial, reclaim an experience of suffering, working to correct the event, transforming the mental state of the practitioner as well as symbolically healing the body of the victimized.

The ritualization of preparing a body and caring for children are actions that cultivate community and family in familiar and seemingly non-radical ways. Neither practice, preparing a body for burial nor caring for children, seems subversive on the surface; these are practices that are non-threatening and often labeled "women's work." In many cultures, tradition dictates women to care for the dead, but the women at the tomb are caring for an executed criminal. This becomes an action that is paradoxically both familiar and subversive. Through an action that is both expected and accepted, these women are actually able to practice resistance against the powers of the empire that killed Jesus.

Similarly, society expects women to care for their children, even when the role includes healing your children from violence you did not perpetrate yourself. The experience of domestic violence subverts the ordinary family structure and often obstructs women from caring for or protecting their children because of the threats of violence coming from the outside and uncontrollable source of the abusive partner. Survivors of abuse, who are protecting and raising their children, are practicing both the expected gender-role as well as subverting it. A mother who becomes her child's healer and protector is both embracing her "duty" as a mother and rejecting the patriarchal stereotype of women's submission to the head of the household. At the House of Peace, the burden of motherhood becomes a practice of hope that imagines a new way of living out what it means to be "family."

Recall Pineda-Madrid's "practices of resistance" from the previous chapter. The community of Ciudad Juárez used public acts of protest, marching, and art to bring attention to the injustices and corruptions that allowed the feminicide to happen and continue to happen. These practices also enacted hope, by re-imagining and embodying the future. Unlike the public acts of protest Pineda-Madrid outlines, here is an example of a mundane, everyday life event that can become subversive and healing in practice. By taking back the caring and protective practices they were unable to perform during their abusive relationship, the women of House of Peace reclaim their roles as mothers and work to heal their children. They are saying "yes" to healing and embracing the difficult road ahead.

"They Trust in an Encounter with God": The Presence of God

"They had been saying to one another, 'Who will roll away the stone for us from the entrance to the tomb?' When they looked up, they saw that the stone, which was very large, had already been rolled back. As they entered the tomb, they saw a young man, dressed in a white robe, sitting on the right side; and they were alarmed."

MARK 16:3-5

"They trust that [House of Peace] is a place where they can find God. Somehow, they see us as that place. So, it's not just a place of dignity it's a place of consolation, but it's a place also where they trust in an encounter with

God. Part of that is just because of the style of relating very intimately, very family like, partly it is the fact that we encourage this to be a community of support, we eat together, we struggle together, we pray together, they share their burden with one another."

AIDA SEGURA, DIRECTOR OF HOUSE OF PEACE

The titular characteristic of the Empty Tomb in Mark's narrative is that Jesus does not make an appearance and instead the women face the absence of Jesus' body and the presence of a stranger, the young man. How do we understand the absence of Jesus in this moment? Does this signal an absence of God's power and presence in a crucial moment of trauma? For theologians and people investigating suffering, healing, and atonement, the presence and role of God in both the crucifixion and resurrection have been central questions. Where is God while Jesus suffers on the cross? Individuals may ask in moments of suffering, "where is God when I suffer?" The House of Peace "Resurrection Stories" address this question, depicting God's presence in a number of ways that can help illuminate why the Empty Tomb is not empty of God's presence, and is actually a helpful depiction of God in the midst of suffering. For many of the women at House of Peace, their relationships with others make God's presence known. This presence shifts and grows throughout their time at the shelter and throughout their healing. As we bring the experiences of the survivors at House of Peace into juxtaposition with the Empty Tomb narrative, the women disciples at the tomb fill the empty space and in relationship embody the presence of God for each other.

Many of the House of Peace "Resurrection Stories" use imagery that depicts God's active nature in the lives of the women, providing resources, people, and opportunities for them in very real and concrete ways. A number of the narratives talk about the friendships and relationships the women make at the shelter, speaking of the other women as "put there" by God to help provide them peace and wisdom. Many of the survivors believe the healthy relationships, people, and opportunities they have experienced since coming to House of Peace are gifts or blessings from God intended for them. The idea that God is providing space, people, and opportunities for the women of House of Peace is a theme in several of the "Resurrection Stories." One story, displayed with a blue cross depicting a dove and rays of light, reflects the role of God through the imagery of God's "guiding hand."[22] In this narrative, God is an active force that guides this woman towards peace and hope after her experience of abuse and suffering. This woman's imaginative interpretation of her experience of the presence of others as connected to her relationship with God, helps her to re-imagine the presence of God in her moments of suffering.

For others writing the "Resurrection Stories," these opportunities and relationships discovered at the house are direct signs and angelic interpreters from God. One woman recounts, "God has always blessed me with angels that take care of me and put such beautiful things along my path."[23] In addition to the "Resurrection Stories," several of the women I interviewed used angelic language, describing messengers of God, to refer to the people who played important roles in their healing journeys. One woman I spoke with, Mariana, reflected on her own anxiety and the fear she felt about her family's move to House of Peace. She was at a loss for how to explain the transition to her children. But she found that the people she met at the house became important relationships in her life. She explained to me, "Truly these people God puts them in the way, they are angels that God sends and puts them on your path to be there when one more needs them, it was very nice to meet so many people, I never thought of meeting so many people with a big heart."[24] Mariana understood God as taking an active and purposeful role in her healing process, through the presence, support and insights of those around her. The people who helped her on her healing journey and the relationships she cultivated at the house came as a surprise to her—almost miraculous—in their unprecedented nature. They were figures of divine intervention or angelic interpreters sent by God.

There is a strong sense from many of the women that the friendships made at the house are divinely intended for their recovery and ability to move forward. These new friendships and figures of support are special, and this type of religious imagery and language signifies this uniqueness. Mariana, later in the same conversation, when prompted about the most important relationships for her healing process, said, "For me the most important person is God because thanks to him he put other people who are around me and who could help me."[25] Mariana, as well as several of

---

22. House of Peace, "Finding Spiritual Strength."

23. House of Peace, "My Cross: The Joy of Living."

24. Mariana, interviewed by Ashley Theuring.

25. Mariana, interviewed by Ashley Theuring.

the other women interviewed, attribute their healing process and the opportunities they experienced at House of Peace as connected to the activity of the Divine in their lives, specifically, as acts of God intended for them.

Another woman I spoke with, Abril, also experienced and expressed God's intentions for her healing. In a moment of despair from her abuse, an acquaintance of her daughter's approached Abril and told her about the House of Peace. The acquaintance gave her the director's contact information and Abril recounted, "and when I see the lady I believe that she was sent from heaven because at that moment I was in a very difficult situation."[26] Abril experienced the acquaintance's compassion and outreach as divinely sent. Similarly, another "Resurrection Story" describes the House of Peace as an opportunity to experience love intended by God. She writes, "When I arrived at the House of Peace and began to share in the community, living with others, I realized that God was giving me an opportunity to live in a place full of love and feeling the presence of the Divine." She concludes, "I have learned to value myself as a woman and understand that God has never abandoned us. Now I feel blessed and loved by God."[27] In this narrative, God actively presents a safe and loving space for this survivor to heal, grow, and strengthen her own self-image.

Following this lead, we can re-imagine the Empty Tomb narrative in the same way. The women present in the tomb, along with the young man, become symbols of the divine presence, will, or intervention in that moment of despair. As we bring this imaginative lens from the testimonies of House of Peace to Mark's narrative of the Empty Tomb, we are able to locate God in the exact moment of divine absence. When the women arrive at the tomb, they are first faced with the obstacle of the large stone blocking their access to Jesus' body. The stone has already been moved. Upon entering the tomb, the women find the tomb empty, except for a young man sitting on the right side. The action of the stone being rolled back happens outside the audience's vision, so whether divine intervention, the young man, or both moved the stone is unknown. What we do know from the narrative is that the Empty Tomb is far from empty. Along with the three women, who came to care for Jesus' body, there is a young man, making a total of four people gathered inside the tomb. While Mark's narrative does not call the young man an angel, the description of the young man and his pattern of his speech all point to his angelic

26. Abril, interviewed by Ashley Theuring.

27. House of Peace, "My Cross: Transformation."

nature.[28] Also, his presence and the presence of the other women echo the House of Peace stories of accompaniment. While the presence of the young man startles the women, and they ultimately leave the tomb in fear, his appearance and message are both hopeful for interpreting their future. Because of his description as a youth, we can assume his presence does not threaten the women, but rather amazes them. Both the removal of the stone and the presence of the young man seem to be of a divine order, events God intends for the mourning women. In the same way, the women at House of Peace experience the people and opportunities that come into their lives during their time at the shelter as divinely sent.

Rather than an empty tomb and an absent God (or the supernatural events depicted in later gospels accounts), the women of House of Peace understand God to be present to them in their healing. God accompanies them in the spaces, people, and opportunities that move them towards hope. Neither an absent God nor a God who miraculously intervenes speaks to the experience of domestic violence. The survivors I interviewed and the House of Peace "Resurrection Stories" reveal God in the presence of others in moments of suffering and trauma. These narratives suggest hope after domestic violence is not miraculously bestowed upon survivors, but rather cultivated in the presence of others. Unlike the community of Mark, who believed they were awaiting the end of time, the women of House of Peace experience a hope that is anchored in the present and transformative for the future.

"We Can Make Those Dreams Happen": Opening the Future

"But he said to them, 'Do not be alarmed; you are looking for Jesus of Nazareth, who was crucified. He has been raised; he is not here. Look, there is the place they laid him. But go, tell his disciples and Peter that he is going ahead of you to Galilee; there you will see him, just as he told you.'"

MARK 16:6–7

"What gives me hope is that we are all here for a purpose. But we must look for that purpose and not to remain like wherever the wind takes us . . . For me, I say that if I continue with my goals, with what my purpose is, I won't be

28. See Marcus, *Mark 8–16*, 1085. Being clad in white, sitting on the right side of the tomb, and his reassuring command, all signal an angelic presence.

just a statistic of someone who gave up or who suffered violence and stayed there . . . Being here has opened my eyes to say that as a human being if you work on what your purpose is you can achieve it. It made me see that God made us so perfect, and He also gives us so many dreams. And we can make those dreams happen. If we work on them we can achieve them."

GABRIELLE, FORMER RESIDENT OF HOUSE OF PEACE

The young man inside the tomb tells the mourning women that Jesus has been raised and he has gone ahead of them to Galilee. While the women are ultimately unable to finish preparing Jesus' body, they are promised that they will see Jesus again in the future. On the face of it, Mark's Empty Tomb narrative offers a less triumphant account than other resurrection narratives, but the young man's message is still hope-filled. This message opens the futures of the women in new ways, which were not possible before coming to the tomb. Hope is transformative. It opens the future to new possibilities, before, unimagined. The young man's message announces a future event—a *proyecto historico,* in the words of Isasi-Diáz as seen in the previous chapter—of seeing and being with Jesus in Galilee. This is a promised future that will require work and action on the part of the women. This hoped-for future is a liberating alternative to the moment of suffering, fear, and persecution the women find themselves in when they meet this young man. For the women at the tomb, the young man's message works to denounce, rather than deny, the current situation of the women. They are told to not be alarmed, and then he names Jesus as the one "who was crucified." Both of these things happen before the young man declares Jesus' resurrection (Mark 16:6). Most significantly, the women do not respond with immediate relief and hope, but rather are silent and scared for a bit longer. This community does not, and cannot, immediately understand the resurrection, but rather they must mourn and name their experience of suffering in witnessing the crucifixion of Jesus.

The "Resurrection Stories" and testimonies of the women at House of Peace stretch the hopeful message presented in the Empty Tomb account even further. While the hopeful message in the Empty Tomb account is more direct and presented by a divine messenger, the accounts of the survivors of House of Peace are subtler and more diverse. The time, space, people, and practices of House of Peace work in a similar way as the message of the young man at the tomb. They open the possible futures of the women who are healing from domestic violence. Most significantly, the experiences and people that help the women to re-imagine their futures are ordinary, mundane aspects of life. For one survivor, Abril, the practice of the "Resurrection Stories" project itself helped her to think more openly about her future. She described the process of painting the cross and writing the narrative during my interview with her. Reaching for words, she wrestled with the significance of her creative process. She highlighted a number of ways the "Resurrection Stories" project helped her own healing process. First, Abril reported that the project gave her space to reflect on her experience and how she was feeling, giving her an interpretive space to narrate her own story. She noted the importance of this, telling me, "there are times that you don't think about how you're feeling."[29] Second, this project gave her an opportunity to reflect on her own situation at the moment of the painting and writing. She noted that in that moment "you realize that you are actually well and you have no problems."[30] Abril expressed that in the space of writing her narrative and painting her cross she experienced a sense of peace or wellbeing. The hope that opened Abril's future in this case did not come from an outside source, but rather herself.

For Abril, her open outlook on the world was a change from when she first came to House of Peace. Her own worldview shifted throughout her healing process. In our interview, she wondered about how the "Resurrection Stories" might be different if the residents wrote them when they first entered House of Peace rather than near the middle to the end of their stay. Abril thought out loud about the difference, "If I had done [the "Resurrection Story"] at first, I think I would have written very different things, but when we did it in the middle of our time at the House of Peace I felt different, I felt calm with myself."[31] Abril continued to describe her state of mind upon first entering the House of Peace and believed her anger would have been much more visible in her "Resurrection Story." But by the time she designed her cross and wrote her narrative, she described her emotional state as much different. "I felt peaceful and looking forward. I felt like that, thinking positive things. I [think] that if we had had that same program when we arrived . . . I think that we should have done another one in the end, so they could see the difference

29. Abril, interviewed by Ashley Theuring.
30. Abril, interviewed by Ashley Theuring.
31. Abril, interviewed by Ashley Theuring.

of how one comes and how we leave."[32] For Abril, the time and daily life at the House of Peace opened her future in a way that had not been possible within her abusive relationship. And she was able to narrate and express this sentiment through the "Resurrection Stories" project.

Abril's experience of her own shifting worldview throughout her stay at House of Peace is an example of the importance of space and time in cultivating hope. In Abril's case, the community of House of Peace provided this space and time. The development of the *proyecto historico,* or a hoped-for future, acknowledges the need for us to denounce suffering and name the evil experienced, before we can announce the open future. House of Peace, as an intentional community, creates a space in which the women are able to work together over time to name their experiences. What Abril's account reveals about hope is that we cultivate hope within our everyday experiences and lived moments. While the message given by the young man in the Empty Tomb narrative is ultimately hopeful, denouncing the crucifixion and announcing the resurrection, the experiences of the survivors at House of Peace show us that this message of hope can come from a multitude of places including oneself and our daily lives.

"It Happens in the Kitchen and the Halls": A Fragile Resurrection

"So they went out and fled from the tomb, for terror and amazement had seized them; and they said nothing to anyone, for they were afraid."

MARK 16:8

"I would [want to] capture the subtleness of what is happening in a person's life when they are here . . . It happens in the kitchen and the halls. You see these women healing each other, and sometimes their children. Just embracing their children for a long time and asking them for forgiveness or telling them they love them . . . But it's very dynamic, so you see the suffering that has—I wouldn't say a purpose, necessarily—but it's part of a kind of new life emerging . . . Once they kind of acknowledge their pain and their woundedness. When they go into it they are really starting to move, create movement in the spirit, I feel. By just acknowledging is a way of validating themselves

32. Abril, interviewed by Ashley Theuring.

by visiting the pain. And sometimes it's pain that has been there a long time."

AIDA SEGURA, DIRECTOR OF HOUSE OF PEACE

Mark's Empty Tomb account ends with the three women fleeing the tomb in terror and amazement after receiving the message from the young man. The young man gives them a message of hope, and yet in this moment, there remains a sense of fear and doubt. While biblical scholars debate the meaning and understanding of this final line for Mark and Mark's community,[33] the simplest interpretation is that these women are left in a state of unease and the terror of the crucifixion remains with them. These women have experienced a harrowing past few days: witnessing the execution of Jesus, following his body to the tomb, presumably being questioned on their connections to their friend and teacher, waking up early in the morning to care for his body, and, ultimately, finding the tomb empty except for an unknown young man. These events would have been a lot to process and the message from the young man would not have undone the traumatic aspects of these previous experiences. The hope related to resurrection and healing does not negate experiences of suffering. As we saw in the theologies of Ivone Gebara and Nancy Pineda-Madrid in the previous chapter, the crucifixion and resurrection are two sides of our everyday reality and both are unending. One does not fully dispel the other. The Empty Tomb presents us with an alternative narrative: a fragile resurrection moment. This fragile resurrection leaves room for the integration of the suffering experienced by these women. Rather than reading this ending as pessimistic or despairing, the open-endedness and jarring conclusion of the Empty Tomb narrative in Mark can represent an imaginative narrative space, which asks the audience to remember the trauma of the crucifixion (and their own traumas) even as it tries to pull them forward with a call to discipleship.

Similar to the fragile resurrection of the Empty Tomb, the narratives of hope and healing I heard at House of Peace did not fully overwrite experiences of suffering. The experiences of domestic violence remained part of the survivors' narratives even after their time at House of Peace. We can see this most evident in the "Resurrection Stories," many of which include images and metaphors of both suffering and healing. Several of

---

33. See chapter 3 above. Also see Billings, "The End of Mark's Gospel," 54; Joynes, "The Sound of Silence," 18; Sawicki, "Making Jesus," 163–65; and Mitchell, *Beyond Fear and Silence*, 2.

"Resurrection Stories" depict symbols of transformation, which represent both sides of the narrative, death and resurrection, in one symbol. One displays the symbol of the butterfly, a symbol that Christians have historically utilized to represent the resurrection of Jesus and the promise of resurrection. The narrative next to this cross explains that the survivor chose the symbol of the butterfly "because it represents for [her] the transformation in [her] life. [Her] resurrection is like the butterflies that have transformed until they can fly and have a new horizon to explore."[34] The symbol of the butterfly connects to both the story of the cross and resurrection and the lived experience of abuse and healing by using a natural and easily recalled example of a caterpillar transforming into a butterfly. The caterpillar is utterly destroyed inside its chrysalises. But in following the narrative structure of its DNA, the caterpillar becomes something completely different, forever marked by this experience. The experience of suffering and death is never completely overwritten, rather it is incorporated into the new imagined future. The crucifixion shapes the resurrection. In this same way, domestic violence is an experience that will continue to shape the women at House of Peace and their stories of hope and healing reflect that reality.

Another symbol of transformation used by the "Resurrection Stories" is the symbol of grapes becoming wine (or raisins). One narrative displayed next to a blue and green cross with a cluster of purple grapes at its center reads, "The grapes symbolize life transformations for me, the changes that turn grapes into wine or even raisins. Even though the grapes change shape, texture, and flavor, they continue being food that nourishes. The same for us: our experiences transform us but our essence remains the same."[35] For this survivor, her lived experience has been a process of transformation, symbolized by both the cross and grapes. This experience has transformed her, but she also remains connected to both the person before and after her experience of abuse. The hope and healing in this metaphor is not something completely new, unconnected to what came before. Rather, her resurrection is a fragile shift into the present, towards the future, deeply rooted in the past.

When we read Mark's Empty Tomb alongside the narratives of House of Peace, the terror and fear of the women at the tomb can be understood as part of the natural process of trauma healing. Resurrection cannot

34. House of Peace, "My Cross: Transformation."
35. House of Peace, "My Cross: The Grapevine, Love, and Life."

come too soon, or it will fail to be fully integrated with the experience of crucifixion. Mark's Empty Tomb account depicts a fragile resurrection message, one that remembers the crucifixion and does not overwrite the suffering experienced by these women. While the narrative ends before these women begin their journey towards healing, integration, and resurrection, the audience does get to witness the first step. These women seek out time, space, and community to mourn their loss and practice discipleship and solidarity by remaining with the crucified. In the same ways that the survivors of House of Peace sought out the healing space of the shelter, the women disciples come to the tomb to practice hope. They planned to embody their hope by caring for Jesus' corpse, and being present to his body and each other. They wanted to imagine a different way of experiencing Jesus' death. Through their agency and their practice of caring for the dead, the women of the tomb gain access to God through each other, the young man, and his message. If the survivors of House of Peace had not chosen to leave their abusive relationships, they may never have experienced the healing and resurrection that they did. Had these women, survivors and disciples, not practiced hope and agency, they may have missed their moments of fragile resurrection completely.

Reimagining the Resurrection: New Revelations of Hope

As we see above, the residents of House of Peace and their narratives expand the practices and concepts of hope developed in the previous chapters of this book. My aim, in scaffolding the stories, voices, and experiences of House of Peace with the narrative of the Empty Tomb, was to allow the House of Peace case study to further resonate with the resurrection narrative, challenging and building an understanding of hope from the context of domestic violence. At the beginning of this chapter, I set out to expand Serene Jones' understanding of the Empty Tomb as an "unending," which allows space for contemplation and imagination. The women of House of Peace, their stories and experiences of domestic violence and healing, have illuminated and revealed a re-imagined Empty Tomb narrative. By sharing their experiences of community and the significance of healthy relationships, they give us deeper and more imaginative ways of reading Mark.

What has surfaced most significantly in these accounts are three major claims about the nature of hope after domestic violence. First, hope in the wake of domestic violence names and denounces crucifixion and suffering while simultaneously embodying a hoped-for future. The practices of presence, witness, and mourning, observed in both the survivors of House of Peace and the re-imagined Empty Tomb narrative work to name suffering, denounce that suffering, and point towards a future way of being. Naming and denouncing suffering allows for the announcement of hope, which we develop in the context of particular crucifixions. The hope that we announce is a hoped-for future that we have not yet realized and we perpetually renew and rename. The women of the house, centering on their experiences of both suffering and healing, designed and wrote the "Resurrection Stories" as a practice of hope. The narratives reveal a reframing of domestic violence, naming the suffering and pointing towards the possibility of subverting that particular evil.

Second, hope after domestic violence practices a fragile resurrection, leaving room for doubt and continued suffering in our lived experience. This hope maintains an open view of the future, but leaves room for doubt, embracing the ambiguous nature of our lives in which we experience serial crucifixions and resurrections. This is a hope that recognizes the uncertainty in life and works to cultivate relationality and imagination even within the moments of suffering and crucifixion. The House of Peace narratives do not deny the reality and continued existence of evil, in the same way that Weingarten's "reasonable hope" leaves space for doubt and focuses on action in the present. The "Resurrection Stories" present a practice that works to narrate survivors' lived experiences and leaves room for the expression of doubt.

Finally, relationships, communities, and everyday life mediates hope after domestic violence as part of a worldview infused with the Divine. In moments of crucifixion, the presence and accompaniment of others mediates resurrection. Our human nature as created in the image of God and our access to grace through the Holy Spirit, allows us to be conduits for the presence of God for others in their moments of suffering and crucifixion. Expanding Pineda-Madrid "practices of resistance," survivors can practice hope after domestic violence through obligatory or mundane tasks, like child-care. These everyday practices can become subversive. These practices of survival do not always look like "resistance" and may even look on the surface like submission to gender roles. But for the women at House of Peace, choosing to embrace and care for their children becomes a healing and radical way to object to the abuse that threatened their family's survival.

House of Peace's narratives and "Resurrection Stories" give us a unique opportunity to read Jesus' crucifixion and resurrection through the experiences of survivors of domestic violence. In bringing these accounts together, we can re-imagine the Gospel resurrection account from within the context of House of Peace. In this way, Christian hope revealed in Jesus' resurrection is also revealed and expanded in the hope practices of House of Peace. In light of these findings, I claim that hope after domestic violence is deeply connected to our ability to experience resurrection and can be understood as an "embodied imaginative hope." In the final chapter, we will further explore "embodied imaginative hope," bringing its insights to bear on the nature of resurrection, as well as the implications for future conversations in theology and the Church.

5

Embodied Imaginative Hope

IN THIS BOOK, I have argued that hope is uniquely expressed in and through the experiences of women emerging from situations of domestic violence. In my re-imagining of Mark's Empty Tomb in light of the narratives and experience of domestic violence survivors at House of Peace, I argue that hope after domestic violence is an embodied imaginative hope in moments of fragile resurrection. The "Resurrection Stories" of House of Peace and the women gathering together to anoint the body of Jesus in Mark's Empty Tomb, both challenge a singular, extrinsic understanding of the crucifixion and resurrection events. Rather, our everyday experiences of suffering and healing are deeply rooted in the cross and resurrection of Jesus, making them practices capable of sacramentality and, in turn, they are revelatory in their representations of the human-Divine relationship and the presence of God in our suffering. Embodied imaginative hope in moments of fragile resurrection after suffering and violence, that I develop in this book, reveals the power of our deeply sacramental lives, communities, and relationships.

Feminists and theologians concerned with trauma continue to bring the experiences of domestic violence survivors into the theological conversation. But this dialogue remains focused on treating domestic violence as a theological problem and reexamining Christianity's understandings of suffering and salvation in light of domestic violence. Some theologians have even excluded the symbols of the crucifixion and resurrection from their investigations, urging women to search solely outside Christian tradition for sources of healing, because of the long and often toxic history of these symbols.[1] Rather than a rejection of the centrality of the crucifixion and resurrection in the Christian tradition, I propose we expand the tradition itself, turning to theologies of hope, women's experience, scripture and how we can re-imagined these today. I reject the claim that tradition has based Christianity on the glorification of innocent suffering and align myself with theologians, such as Rosemary Radford Ruether, who claim that "Christianity has in it the seeds of an alternative theory, a theory of liberation, equality, and dignity for all persons."[2] Deeply rooted in feminist and trauma conversations, I carry this feminist theological trajectory forward, addressing the practical theological questions domestic violence poses. Specifically, in this book, I asked "how does domestic violence and suffering shape our bodily and communal practices of hope and resurrection?" To answer this, I have argued for an embodied imaginative hope, which reveals that humanity—as the body of Christ—not only participates in healing creation but can embody salvation and hope for ourselves and for each other through witness, support, and presence.

Future Implications

While past theological understandings of hope inform this project, I have pushed the conversation forward academically, pastorally, and theologically, by turning to the voices and experiences of the most marginalized in our country. The concepts and practices of embodied imaginative hope we find at the center of healing after domestic violence reveals a hope that is radical in its ability to name evil and suffering while exploring possible action for the here and now, fragile in its transience, imaginative in its ability to open the future while leaving room for doubt, and embodied by individuals and communities in the mundane tasks of life. Embodied imaginative hope in moments of fragile resurrection has practical implications for daily practices and understanding the role of the Church in healing, as well as large constructive theological implications for themes such as crucifixion and sin.

First, this project reinforces the liberationist call to name and denounce suffering, highlighting the role of witness. In both the House of Peace "Resurrection Stories" and the re-imagined gospel narrative, the

---

1. Brown and Parker, "For God So Loves the World?"
2. Radford Ruether, "The Western Religions Tradition," 40.

role of sharing and hearing testimonies of suffering are crucial parts of healing and being able to practice hope after domestic violence. The practices of witness and story-telling connect individual experiences of crucifixion to a larger reality of suffering in the world, naming and denouncing systemic evils that are antithetical to the hoped-for future. Domestic violence has no place in the Kin-dom of God and we must reject it in the same way that the resurrection rejects the crucifixion. The future, into which the Divine calls all of us to live, is egalitarian and both women and men will flourish as equals. In order for us to realize this *proyecto historico*, practices of hope must name and denounce the current reality of domestic violence. As revealed in both House of Peace narratives and the re-imagined Empty Tomb narrative, there is a period of mourning, witness, and naming the crucifixion before resurrection. In connecting domestic violence to the crucifixion experience, we do not justify, glorify, or legitimize the suffering of domestic violence, but rather we expose it as injustice. In this same way, we relight Jesus' crucifixion as unjust and rooted in systemic evil.

This project also reveals that our relationships with others mediate hope and resurrection after domestic violence. The practice of accompaniment was central to both the House of Peace and re-imagined gospel narrative. Specifically, the example of building healthy relationships between mothers and children was one practice that revealed the possible depths of human compassion and empathy, even in less than ideal situations. These types of deep, healthy personal relationships in our lives mimic the type of relationship God wants with us. In this same way, those who help us to practice hope in our times of suffering mediate the presence of God in those moments. In both the Empty Tomb and House of Peace narratives, those who are present in our darkest moments reveal the presence of God. For the women of House of Peace, the people who accompanied them through their healing process—the director, the other women at the house, the larger community, and their children—were the companions that helped them to move them towards healing. The House of Peace "Resurrection Stories" even highlighted the importance of strengthening the self in order for healing to take place. In the re-imagined Empty Tomb narrative, the women find the tomb empty of Jesus' body, but they also find a space filled with possibility, each other, and the young man with his message of hope. In both cases, Jesus' resurrection and the healing process after domestic violence, our relationships with ourselves and each other mediate resurrection.

Finally, hope after domestic violence is accessible through embodied, imaginative practices that allow practitioners to cultivate their own sense of agency from their embattled positions within situations of suffering. In this world, we do not experience resurrection and hope once and for all, rather we find more transient hope in our daily lives. In those moments of fragile resurrection, survivors can practice embodied imaginative hope, even though suffering and crucifixion may still be part of their lives. Our relationships with others mediate hope, and in order to access that hope we must have agency to practice resurrection. All of these aspects of hope after domestic violence together paint a picture of a process of healing and resurrection that is ongoing, based in healthy relationships, community oriented, and embodied. How are the academy, the church, and the field of theology to move forward with this knowledge about the nature of hope after domestic violence?

Impact on the Academy:
Beyond Awareness

In this book, I build off the foundation laid by feminist thinkers over the last forty years, such as Rosemary Radford Ruether, Marie Fortune, and Judith Herman, by reading the experience of domestic violence as a theological problem. The theological responses of these thinkers focused on naming the problem of domestic violence, pointing to the role of the perpetrator, problematic atonement theories that glorified suffering, the poor responses and lack of education of the clergy, and the silence of the community. I hope this book will move the conversation forward by investigating current and contextual practices of healing after trauma, therefore, contributing to the academic fields of feminist, trauma, and practical theologies.

Much of my work in this book has been possible through a sacramental approach to practical theology, in which lived experience is not only an important dialogue partner for theological investigation but central to our ability to access God. Both practical theology and Catholic theology support a sacramental worldview, seeing our daily lives and practices as external signs of internal truths. While not all practices or actions are "Sacraments," God infuses creation with God's self; God created us in the image of God's self and connected us to the Holy Spirit, allowing for human experience and reason to be a source of revelation. Trauma theology has always been situated in the lived experience of trauma, but this book engages particular practices as possible sources of theological revelation, turning specifically to the practices of resurrection at House of Peace and the Empty Tomb narrative for theological insight.

Continuing the feminist theological conversation around domestic violence forward, I chose to stay within one context for the research that underlines this book, that of House of Peace. In order to move beyond diagnoses, I turned to current responses and practices of a community wrestling to find hope, healing, and resurrection in the wake of domestic violence. Expanding both the feminist and womanist conversations by looking at the modern-day experience of Latina survivors of domestic violence in Chicago, this project would not have been possible without the past decades of feminist and womanist work to expose the problems of domestic violence and the importance of context in shaping these experiences. The particular "crucifixion" that is the experience of domestic violence calls for an equally particular understanding of "resurrection." I turned to the suffering and healing narratives of the survivors at House of Peace in order to re-imagine a feminist reading of the Gospel of Mark's Empty Tomb, uncovering a resurrection and hope in light of domestic violence. This re-imagining allows us to bring several theological aspects of hope and resurrection to light, which will in turn shape how we practice hope and resurrection into the future.

In this book, I also uphold and follow a methodology informed by a preferential option for the poor, which is central to both Catholic and feminist theologies. Trauma theologians have always engaged the voices and experiences of the traumatized and this book continues to develop this ethical norm, incorporating the *mujerista* and womanist privileging of the voices of women of color and investigating the role of race and class in experiences of trauma and healing. Liberation and Catholic theologians have highlighted the necessary centrality of the "crucified ones" in the Christian tradition and this project pushes trauma theology to consider the preferential option for the poor as a theological norm and central part of discerning which experiences of trauma we should privilege in theological investigations. The women of House of Peace, as mostly Latina, immigrant women, are particularly susceptible to violence and face a number of barriers in their healing processes particular to their race and class. Rather than investigating trauma as a universal experience, absent of its context, I push trauma theology to consider the contextual shaping of trauma. Feminist and womanist scholars have called on their white colleagues to pay attention to the contextual particulars of trauma, and I hope this book responds to that call.

One key contribution this project makes to future feminist theological responses to domestic violence is that we must go beyond the education of our clergy. The entire Church, the body of Christ, must be involved in the practice of resurrection. An individual pastor in a community cannot provide the type of ongoing, relational, and community support that survivors of domestic violence, or anyone, need to experience and practice hope. Domestic violence isolates and diminishes individuals, disconnecting survivors from themselves, others, and God. In order for us to restore those relationships, an entire community must help individuals practice hope. A singular, internal event of individual strength and grit is not healing or resurrection; we are not resurrected once and for all, but rather must live into resurrection in our communities. By this same token, this is not the sole responsibility of one clergy person; the Christian community—as the Body of Christ—must work together to create a context in which domestic violence is neither tolerated nor ignored. It is not just the work of a few elite leaders, but rather the work of whole communities.

Impact on Theology: Rethinking the Cross

My construction of embodied imaginative hope out of the fragile resurrection of both the Markan gospel and the women of House of Peace impacts how we understand the cross. In chapter 3, I began with women's multiple experiences of the cross and expanded this idea to the resurrection narrative. Now, I return to the cross with the insights we have garnered from the theological idea of embodied imaginative hope. The re-imaging of hope and resurrection, I have put forth, implies a reading of the crucifixion that expands beyond the cross of Jesus. The fragile resurrection insinuates a fragile crucifixion, where hope seeps into the wood of the cross, not through the justification or glorification of the act of suffering itself, but rather because of its impermanence. A reading of the crucifixion shaped by the imaginative hope of the resurrection, allows us to see God's presence even in the very moment of crucifixion. The presence and agency of the women who stood at the foot of the cross hints at the future resurrection in the same way their steadfastness at the empty tomb carries the trauma of the crucifixion into that space. The claims about hope, resurrection, and salvation at the center of this project certainly hint at future theological explorations of suffering, crucifixion, and sin.

Often, popular theologies of the cross treat Jesus' crucifixion as a singular event outside the context of history. In the imaginations of many Christian, Jesus' death on a cross was an inevitable part of God's plan, rather than a result of Jesus' life and mission. This theological line of thought ignores the reality that Jesus' death, the execution of a criminal under the Roman Empire, was contextual and driven by systemic evil. As we saw in the example of the suffering servant and the crucified people, the cross is a reality that has been repeated throughout history before and after Jesus. Developing a Christian understanding of crucifixion that looks beyond the single context of Jesus, the same way that resurrection is understood in this project, may allow us to name evil and suffering more precisely and remove God's problematic role in the death of his child. My proposed expansion of our understanding of crucifixion does not make Jesus' death any less significant in the Christian tradition, but rather, strengthens its importance by connecting it to contextual moments throughout all of history. Jesus' death is not significant because it is superlative in its tragedy, its violence, or its loss. Rather Jesus' death is significant for Christians because it mirrors the historical reality faced by all those closest to God, the crucified people.

"Fragile resurrection" incorporates women's experience of suffering and domestic violence, acknowledging that resurrection is ongoing and not once and for all. Similarly, this points to a more fragile understanding of the crucifixion; a "fragile crucifixion" does not have the final word and is transient in nature, coming and going at different times in our lives. Change is the only constant and the mercurial nature of our lives is bitter-sweet. Moments of joy and suffering are both equally likely to fade overtime. If resurrection is not a singular and extrinsic event, neither is crucifixion. In our lived experience, we are neither free from suffering nor is it totalizing; crucifixion is also not once and for all. We can re-imagine the crucifixion as something that stretches both into the past and future, beyond Jesus' context. In the same way that the resurrection must leave room for doubt, moments of crucifixion, even in the depths of despair, hint at other possibilities. At Jesus' execution, an act the Roman Empire intended to be a terrorizing display of hopelessness, Jesus' friends and family defiantly chose to be present with him. Even after his death, the women disciples chose to care for his body. A fragile crucifixion means that even in our despair we can practice hope and imagine different ways of being. In their refusal to give into the Roman Empire's insistence that they and their loved ones did not matter, the women at the empty tomb embodied a new way of imagining community. In a similar way, the women of House of Peace refused to be crushed by the societal powers of sexism, racism, and classism, and came together to re-imagine what it meant to live as a family and community.

When we re-imagine the cross in these ways, we can see more clearly the role that the community and others play in crucifixion. In the same way that others mediate the resurrection and healing, we are all implicated in crucifixion. Suffering and systemic evil is not the result of a single sin or villain, but in the same way that we mediate healing and the Divine in the world, humanity has the capacity to fail at this mediation. And when we fail at living into our divine calling, we do damage to creation and each other. As hope is accessible and often practiced through the mundane, crucifixion is also prevalent and is fueled by the choices we make in our daily lives. This re-imagining of crucifixion hints at our possibility as individuals and communities to do harm, reframing the way we think about sin, guilt, and evil. Most importantly, this fragile crucifixion complicates the way we think about atonement and God's role in suffering—a deeper theological revelation I hope to explore in future works.

Impact on Churches:
Practical and Pastoral

The communal nature of hope, that I have highlighted throughout this book, reveals an important role that church communities have to play in responding to domestic violence and suffering as a wider reality. Specifically, the community mediates resurrection and without the larger "Body of Christ" playing a role in practicing resurrection, the Church cannot function in its role to mediate salvation. The Church, as a community of people, has always been called to practice and mediate resurrection. As the body of Christ and an important source of hope, the Church community must practice resurrection, or it fails as the Church. Healing after trauma is not the job of an individual, nor is it feasible for only a few key players, such as pastors, to carry this burden for the entire community. Rather, if the Church is to truly mediate salvation, the larger community must practice resurrection. As we saw in earlier chapters, church communities' responses to domestic violence have focused on clergy and leadership training. But this book calls for a more holistic and communal response to trauma healing.

This is not to say that all church communities need to incorporate the specific practice of the "Resurrection Stories" from House of Peace. Practices of hope are as contextual as suffering and salvation. Each community must discern how they can embody hope. This job requires naming and diagnosing the suffering and crucifixions of each particular community. Also, this discerning process is never ending. Communities change and the problems they face also change. The Church, as the body of Christ, must adapt and discern, naming suffering and practicing resurrection over and over with every new crucifixion. Each church community must begin and continue the hard work of discernment, naming the suffering in their community and responding to those crucifixions with practices of resurrection and hope, reshaping their community. Will this lead to the decentering of pastoral practices like worship or mass, weakening any sense of a universal Church? This and other questions point to the important future work this project has exposed. For churches who practice the Eucharist, the communion meal can be a core symbol of the human-Divine relationship mediated through the Church's unity and will continue to function as the central example of the sacramental reality of the world. The Eucharist can help to ground a community in an ever-shifting sacramental landscape. But church communities must make a renewed effort to practice embodied imaginative hope in moments of fragile resurrection in order for the "Body of Christ" to embody the Kin-dom of God and respond to the daily crucifixions of the most vulnerable in their communities.

Embodied Imaginative Hope

What does embodied imaginative hope look like for our current context of trauma and isolation? How do we and survivors of trauma practice hope in the wake of a pandemic, and in the midst of political, racial, economic, and ecological crises? To begin answering these questions, in the last chapter, I argued for three major aspects of hope, which we found in the dialogue between survivor testimonies from House of Peace and Mark's Gospel Empty Tomb narrative. First, hope must take time to name and denounce evil, while also exploring the present for ways of embodying resistance to these evils. Second, hope does not exclude doubt, nor ignore the possibility of returned or continued suffering. And third, we mediate hope to ourselves and others in our everyday lives. As I have argued throughout this book, hope is contextually dependent. And we must take this into consideration when we explore embodied imaginative hope and its practice in the wake of domestic violence in our current situation of COVID-19, quarantine, civil unrest, economic downturn, and political uncertainty. Our current context greatly influences the type of suffering experienced by survivors, which in turn shapes the response. For example, globally, there has been a calculated rise in domestic violence and the tactics used by abusers are evolving to fit the current crisis.[3]

Identifying Evil and Exploring What Is Possible Today

Those practicing embodied imaginative hope must take time and space to name the specific evil and suffering perpetrated against them. We cannot move to healing or resurrection without identifying and understanding to some extent the roots of our suffering. So, what does this mean for the practice of hope after domestic violence in our current context? We must consider the unique facets of daily life that survivors face *today*. The first glaring aspect of our current context is the public response to the 2020 pandemic. Coronavirus, COVID-19, and the ensuing public health crisis, have required us to engage in practices of social distancing, quarantining, and mass stay-at-home orders. All of these practices are meant to isolate us physically from each other to avoid the spread of virus, but have also caused families and individuals to become socially isolated. Pre-COVID, many abusers used tactics to isolate their partners from friends, family, and other social supports, but under quarantine this type of isolation is a part of all our daily lives. Not only does this isolation make it more dangerous for survivors currently in abusive relationships, by limiting their support systems and options to leave a relationship, but it can retraumatize survivors who are no longer in an active relationship with their abusive partner. Stay-at-home orders can keep survivors from connecting to their healing communities, or even retrigger feelings of isolation and hopelessness.

3. See Nogushi, "Domestic Abuse Can Escalate"; and Taub, "A New Covid-19 Crisis."

Another unique aspect of our current context is that for a number of reasons, the United States has also faced a skyrocketing unemployment rate and an economic downturn that experts believe may result in the worst recession in nearly a century, during this same timeframe of pandemic. The severity of domestic violence has often been correlated with economic stress in a household. In addition, lack of financial resources can make it impossible for a survivor to leave or stay separated from their partner for long. Abusers have historically used finances to control their partners, and today the instability of employment makes it much easier to keep that control.

Another distinctive characteristic of our current context is that our society has become more integrated with technology and dependent on the internet. The increasing daily use of online services, especially under the conditions of quarantine, has encompassed everything from groceries to banking, to school and work. The ability to accomplish necessary daily tasks from home is extremely beneficial for many, but unfortunately has hidden consequences for survivors of abuse. The more integrated our lives become with technology, the easier they are to hijack, stalk, and control.[4] For example, a survivor may be separated from their abuser, but their abuser can access their bank account, online bills, or other online profiles.

Our current context is also defined by increasing divisions in political and social issues. At the time of writing this, the United States has been rocked by a summer of protests after the brutal murder of George Floyd at the hands of police. Issues around race and police brutality are at the forefront of every political discussion, on top of the political and social stressors that the response to COVID-19 has brought. In the past, studies have shown that civil unrest increases the likelihood of violent households in the future.[5] This is not to say we should not fight for reform, through protests and political battles. In fact, I believe the exact opposite is true. Many of us have neglected these issues, like racial and gender inequality, to such an extent in our country that "reform" doesn't seem to address the deeper problems. But the struggle and unrest that results from this work may have unforeseen consequences for survivors of domestic violence.

4. See Nogushi, "Domestic Abuse Can Escalate"
5. Gutierrez, and Gallegos, "The Effect of Civil Conflict on Domestic Violence."

How can we name this evil? And what does it look like to actively resist this evil and embody the hoped-for future? The particular evils faced by domestic violence survivors today take the forms of isolation, financial instability, loss of control, and the general instability of our society. These affect many of us in our current era, but domestic violence amplifies the negative effects of all four. As I outlined in chapter 2, the continued privatization of the household allows for the practice of abuse. But through raising awareness and increased public discussions survivors can reconnect, find resources, regain control, and find stability in their lives. Again, the contextual nature of hope may mean that these practices look different for each person, but as a community we can help to create systems that support survivors in their needs to reconnect, find financial stability, regain their autonomy, and feel stable in their future.

An Open but Fragile Future

The understanding that the future is open, for good and bad, roots embodied imaginative hope. We experience moments of fragile resurrection, but suffering may return. Doubt is not the opposite of hope, but rather a characteristic of a robust hope that can sustain itself through the return of trauma. Our lives are ambiguous and the reality is that the future is unknown and, generally, out of our control. This is poignantly felt in our current context. Many of us in the United States, and globally, experienced the spring of 2020 as a tectonic shift from our daily routines. As the country closed down in order to slow the spread of the coronavirus, many people lost their jobs, or were told to work from home; daycares, restaurants, and stores were all closed; and medical personnel were suddenly fighting on the "front lines." Even now, as we begin to reopen, the future remains unknown. When will schools and universities be "normal" again? When will it be safe to send our children to daycare? Will the service industry and all those who work in it be able to rebound from the economic fallout? When the virus continues or worsens, will our first responders receive the support they need? In addition to the response to COVID-19, 2020 has marked a resurgence of public activism for racial justice, which has been met with police brutality and crackdowns. Many people, around the world, filled the streets looking for change and prophesying a new future. With the 2020 elections in the United States, many feel uncertain of what the future holds for us as a country and individuals.

Our current context is overwhelming even in stable households, when we consider the added layer of domestic violence for many, the instability of life becomes almost unbearable. Many survivors are facing job loss, unstable childcare, illness and death, on top of managing an abusive partner, trying to stay safe, and/or planning to leave. As survivors take steps to stabilize their lives in this moment, they are also contending with the shifting landscape of our society and economy. In our current historical moment of change and instability, Miguel A. De La Torre's notion of "hopelessness" helps us to think of practical ways forward.[6] De La Torre argues that by embracing hopelessness, we become free to disrupt society and completely re-imagine what is possible. Rather than "hoping" for things to be different, we accept the brokenness of our society and begin to play in the brokenness. The radical liberative praxis that comes out of hopelessness becomes a possible way towards justice. But De La Torre warns that these acts of defiance can lead to crucifixion and we should not view them with naïve optimism.

When the future is open, but fragile, radical liberative praxis can help us find ways to survive and thrive in the moment. In situations of domestic violence, the privatized, patriarchal household *is* the broken system. But it is not the only choice. Our insistence, thinking that there is a right way to be a partner, mother, and woman create the barriers that survivors face when leaving. Even after escaping domestic violence, survivors face the reality that they may never have the loving, supportive significant other for which they hoped. Their children may never have a healthy father. But the future is open and there is more than one way to have a healthy family. There are ways to re-imagine these relationships of partner and parent, to re-imagine how a household operates, and new ways to embody family. House of Peace is one example of how we can re-imagine these aspects of our lives and embody them through communal living. When the future is unknowable, we become free from the past scripts that have created suffering.

Relational and Accessible

In order to find the energy to break and play with societal scripts that no longer feed us, we can draw inspiration and support from our communities, relationships, and practices of everyday life. We can find hope

---

6. See de la Torre, *Embracing Hopelessness*.

in the seemingly mundane aspects of our lives, because humans and all of creation are infused with the Divine, through principles such as sacramentality, grace, *imago dei*, and the actions of the Holy Spirit. The Divine mediates through creation and the people around us, therefore our practices of healing need not be rare or extraordinary, but can be rooted in the things and people that help us to flourish in the here and now, making hope something that is relational and accessible, even in the midst of suffering.

In our current moment, finding communities of support, building deep relationships, and depending on others are all complicated by practices of social distancing and societal quarantining. The daily practices of avoiding other people, staying home, even maintaining the recommended six-feet of separation, all encourage isolation and self-dependence, at the expense of our communities. There is a growing mistrust of others in public spaces as our knowledge of how the virus spreads grows. The reality of asymptomatic cases makes it so that *anyone* could be a carrier and not know it. As the issue of public health becomes politicized and misinformation spreads, there is a growing division between those who feel we are not doing enough to combat the spread of the virus and those who feel we are doing too much and forgetting to live our lives. Community support and deep relationships are integral to the flourishing of everyone, but particularly important for the healing journey of trauma survivors and specifically survivors of domestic violence. What does community, companionship, and interdependence look like in the midst of social distancing?

The women at House of Peace show us that hope can come from unexpected places and that we can re-imagine even routine practices of survival. Practices of self-care and caring for our dependents can become ways of subverting death-dealing cultural shifts. In response to domestic violence, which reifies the patriarchal household, the women of House of Peace re-imagined their families and found life in reestablishing relationships with their children. Today, as daily routines, jobs, and families continue to experience disruption under quarantine, climate change, and economic and political crises, domestic tasks, self-care routines, and other mundane events can become daily rituals of agency and stability. There can even be a fragile hope in practices that reestablish our means of survival, such as finding financial stability and accessing resources in the community. Practices that embody hope are simple and accessible ways of living into a future that is not yet fully possible. But in their imaginative capacity, these practices of embodied hope are radical, worldbuilding moments in which we say "no" to the status quo of oppression and abuse and "yes" to a future life of flourishing.

Bibliography

Abraham, Susan. "Justice as the Mark of the Catholic Feminist Ecclesiology." In *Frontiers in Catholic Feminist Theology: Shoulder to Shoulder*, edited by Susan Abraham and Elena Procario-Foley, 193–214. Minneapolis: Fortress, 2009.

Abril, Interviewed by Ashley Theuring, House of Peace, Chicago, November 2016.

Adams, Carol J. "Toward a Feminist Theology of Religion and the State." *Theology & Sexuality* 1/2 (1995) 61–83.

———. *Woman-Battering*. Minneapolis: Fortress, 1994.

Aida Segura, Interviewed by Ashley Theuring, House of Peace, Chicago, October 2013.

Ames, Natalie, and Leslie F. Ware. "Latino Protestants: Religion, Culture, and Violence against Women." In *Religion and Men's Violence against Women*, edited by Andy J. Johnson, 149–62. New York: Springer, 2015.

Bachman R, Zaykowski H, Kallmyer R, Poteyeva M, Lanier C. *Violence against American Indian and Alaska Native Women and the Criminal Justice Response: What Is Known*. Washington, DC: National Institute of Justice, 2008.

Baker-Fletcher, Karen. "The Strength of My Life." In *Embracing the Spirit: Womanist Perspectives on Hope, Salvation, and Transformation*, edited by Emilie Townes, 122–39. Maryknoll, NY: Orbis 2015.

Bent-Goodley, T., and K. B. Stennis. "Intimate Partner Violence within Church Communities of African Ancestry." In *Religion and Men's Violence against Women*, edited by Andy J. Johnson, 133–48. New York: Springer, 2015.

Berryman, Phillip. *Liberation Theology: Essential Facts about the Revolutionary Movement in Latin America—and Beyond*. Philadelphia: Temple University Press, 1987.

Beste, Jennifer Erin. *God and the Victim: Traumatic Intrusions on Grace and Freedom*. Oxford: Oxford University Press, 2007.

Billings, Bradly S. "The End of Mark's Gospel and the Markan Community: A Fresh Look in an Old Place." *Colloquium* 46/1 (2014) 42–54.

Black, M. C., K. C. Basile, M. J. Breiding, S. G. Smith, M. L. Walters, M. T. Merrick, J. Chen, and M. R. Stevens, MR. *The National Intimate Partner and Sexual Violence Survey (NISVS): 2010 Summary Report*. Atlanta: National Center for Injury Prevention and Control, Centers for Disease Control and Prevention, 2011.

Bloch, Ernst. *The Principle of Hope*. 3 vols. Translated by Neville Plaice et al. Oxford: Blackwell, 1986.

Boff, Clodovis, and Leonardo Boff. *Introducing Liberation Theology*. Translated by Paul Burns. Maryknoll, NY: Orbis 1987.

Bohn, Carole R. "Dominion to Rule: The Roots and Consequences of a Theology of Ownership." In *Christianity, Patriarchy and Abuse: A Feminist Critique*, edited by Joanne Carlson Brown and Carole R. Bohn, 105–16. New York: Pilgrim, 1989.

Bowker, Lee H. "Religious Victim and Their Religious Leaders: Services Delivered to One Thousand Battered Women by the Clergy." In *Abuse and Religion: When Praying Isn't Enough*, edited by Anne L. Horton and Judith A. Williamson, 235–46. Lexington, MA: Heath, 1988.

Breiding, M. J., S. G. Smith, K. C. Basile, M. L. Walters, J. Chen, and M. T. Merrick. "Prevalence and Characteristics of Sexual Violence, Stalking, and Intimate Partner Violence Victimization—National Intimate Partner and Sexual Violence Survey." *Morbidity and Mortality Weekly Report. Surveillance Summaries* 63/8 (2014) 1–9.

Brink, L., and Deborah Green, eds. *Commemorating the Dead: Texts and Artifacts in Context: Studies of Roman, Jewish, and Christian Burials*. New York: de Gruyter, 2008.

Brinkerhoof, Merlin B., Elaine Grandin, and Eugen Lupri. "Religious Involvement and Spousal Violence: The Canadian Case." *Journal for the Scientific Study of Religion* 31 (1992) 15–31.

Brown, Joanne Carlson, and Carole R. Bohn. "Introduction." In *Christianity, Patriarchy and Abuse: A Feminist Critique*. Edited by Joanne Carlson Brown and Carole R. Bohn. New York: Pilgrim, 1989.

Brown, Joanne Carlson, and Rebecca Parker. "For God So Loves the World?" In *Violence against Women and Children: A Christian Theological Sourcebook*, edited by Carol J. Adams and Marie Fortune, 36–59. London: Black 1995.

Burke, Kevin F. "The Crucified People as 'Light for the Nations': A Reflection on Ignacio Ellacuría." In *Rethinking Martyrdom*, edited by Teresa Okure, Jon Sobrino, and Felix Wilfred. *Concilium* 1 (2003) 123–30.

Burnett, M. N. "Suffering and Sanctification: The Religious Context of Battered Woman's Syndrome." *Pastoral Psychology* 44/3 (1996) 145–49

Bushman, B. J., R. D. Ridge, E. Das, C. W. Key, and G. L. Busath. "When God Sanctions Killing: Effect of Scriptural Violence on Aggression." *Psychological Science* 18 (2007) 204–7.

Cahalan, Kathleen, and Bryan Froehle. "A Developing Discipline." In *Invitation to Practical Theology: Catholic Voices and Visions*, edited by Claire E. Wolfteich, 27–51. New York: Paulist, 2014.

Carr, David McLain. *Holy Resilience: The Bible's Traumatic Origins*. New Haven: Yale University Press, 2014.

Center for Disease Control and Prevention. *National Intimate Partner and Sexual Violence Survey*, 2010.

Chopp, Rebecca S. "Theology and the Poetics of Testimony." *Criterion* (Winter 1998) 2–12.

———. "Practical Theology and Liberation." In *Formation and Reflection: The Promise of Practical Theology*, edited by Lewis S. Mudge and James N. Poling, 120–38. Minneapolis: Fortress, 1987.

Clark, Ron. "Is There Peace within Our Walls? Intimate Partner Violence and White Mainline Protestant Churches in North America." In *Religion and Men's Violence against Women*, edited by Andy J. Johnson, 195–206. New York: Springer, 2015.

Coleman, Monica A. *Making a Way out of No Way: A Womanist Theology*. Minneapolis: Fortress, 2008.

Cooper-White, Pamela. *The Cry of Tamar: Violence against Women and the Church's Response*. Minneapolis: Fortress. 2012.

Copeland M. Shawn. *Enfleshing Freedom: Body, Race, and Being*. Minneapolis: Fortress, 2010.

———. "Wading through Many Sorrows: Toward a Theology of Suffering in Womanist Perspective." In *A Troubling in My Soul: Womanist Perspectives on Evil and Suffering*, edited by Emilie Townes, 109–29. Maryknoll, NY: Orbis, 1993.

———. "Weaving Memory, Structuring Ritual, Evoking Mythos: Commemoration of the Ancestors." In *Invitation to Practical Theology: Catholic Voices and Vision*, edited by Claire Wolfteich, 125–48. New York: Paulist, 2014.

Crawford, Anna Elaine Brown. *Hope in the Holler: A Womanist Theology*. Louisville: Westminster John Knox, 2002.

De'Angelo, Mary Rose. "Unnamed Women at the Cross." In *Women in Scripture: A Dictionary of Named and Unnamed Women in the Hebrew Bible, the Apocryphal/Deuterocanonical Books, and the New Testament*, edited by Carol L. Meyers, Ross Shepard Kraemer, and Toni Craven, 421. Grand Rapids: Eerdmans, 2001.

Dewey, Arthur J. *Inventing the Passion: How the Death of Jesus Was Remembered*. Salem, OR: Polebridge, 2017.

Dillen, Annemie, and Robert Mager. "Research in Practical Theology: Methods, Methodology, and Normativity." In *Invitation to Practical Theology: Catholic Voices and Vision*, edited by Claire Wolfteich, 301–28. New York: Paulist, 2014.

Dobash, R. E., and R. P. Dobash. *Violence against Wives: A Case against the Patriarchy*. New York: Free Press, 1979.

Downey, John K., ed. *Love's Strategy: The Political Theology of Johann Baptist Metz*. Harrisburg, PA: Trinity, 1999.

Doyle, Dominic. "'A Future, Difficult, Yet Possible Good': Defining Christian Hope." In *Hope: Promise, Possibility and Fulfillment*. Edited by Richard Lennan and Nancy Pineda-Madrid. New York: Paulist, 2013.

Ellacuría, Ignacio. "The Crucified People." In *Ignacio Ellacuría: Essays on History, Liberation, and Salvation*, edited by Michael Edward Lee, 195–226. Maryknoll, NY: Orbis 2013.

———. "Discernir 'El Signo' de los Tiempos." In *Escritos Teológicos*, 2:133–35. 2 vols. Colección Teología latinoamericana 25–26. San Salvador: UCA, 2000.

Ellison, Christopher G., and Kristin L. Anderson. "Religious Involvement and Domestic Violence among U.S. Couples." *Journal for the Scientific Study of Religion* 40 (2001) 269–86.

Ellison, Christopher G., John P. Bartawski, and Kristin L. Anderson. "Are There Religious Variations in Domestic Violence?" *Journal of Family Issues* 20 (1999) 87–113.

Empereur, James L., and Eduardo Fernández. *La vida sacra: Contemporary Hispanic Sacramental Theology*. Lanham, MD: Rowman & Littlefield, 2006.

Enns, Diane. *The Violence of Victimhood*. University Park: Pennsylvania State University Press, 2012.

Eugene, Toinnette M. "'Swing Low, Sweet Chariot!': A Womanist Response to Sexual Violence and Abuse." In *Violence against Women and Children: A Christian Theological Sourcebook*, edited by Carol J. Adams and Marie Fortune, 185–200. New York: Continuum, 1998.

Fortune, Marie M. "Forgiveness: The Last Step." In *Abuse and Religion: When Praying Isn't Enough*, edited by Anne L. Horton and Judith A. Williamson, 215–20. Lexington, MA: Heath, 1988.

———. "The Transformation of Suffering." In *Christianity, Patriarchy and Abuse: A Feminist Critique*, edited by Joanne Carlson Brown and Carole R. Bohn. New York: Pilgrim, 1989.

Fortune, Marie M., and James Poling. "Calling to Accountability: The Church's Response to Abusers." In *Violence against Women and Children: A Christian Theological Sourcebook*, edited by Carol J. Adams and Marie Fortune, 451–63. New York: Continuum, 1998.

Fowler, Robert M. *Let the Reader Understand: Reader-Response Criticism and the Gospel of Mark.* Minneapolis: Fortress, 1991.

Francis, Pope. *The Joy of the Gospel: Evangelii Gaudium.* Dublin: Veritas, 2014.

Gaillardetz, Richard. *By What Authority?: A Primer on Scripture, the Magisterium, and the Sense of the Faithful.* Collegville, MN: Liturgical, 2003.

García-Rivera, Alex. "Sacraments: Enter the World of God's Imagination." *U.S. Catholic* 59/1 (1994) 6–12.

Gebara, Ivone, and Maria Clara Bingemer. *Mary: Mother of God, Mother of the Poor.* Translated by Phillip Berryman. Maryknoll, NY: Orbis, 1987.

———. *Out of the Depths: Women's Experience of Evil and Salvation.* Minneapolis: Fortress, 2002.

Gillum, Tameka L., Cris M. Sullivan, and Deborah I. Bybee. "The Importance of Spirituality in the Lives of Domestic Violence Survivors." *Violence against Women* 12 (2006) 240–50.

Griffith, Colleen M. "Christian Hope: A Grace and a Choice." In *Hope: Promise, Possibility and Fulfillment.* Edited by Richard Lennan and Nancy Pineda-Madrid. New York: Paulist, 2013.

Gutierrez, Italo A., and Jose V. Gallegos, "The Effect of Civil Conflict on Domestic Violence: The Case of Peru." Santa Monica, CA: Rand Corporation, 2016. https://www.rand.org/pubs/working_papers/WR1168.html.

Haight, Roger. *An Alternative Vision: An Interpretation of Liberation Theology.* 1985. Reprint, Eugene, OR: Wipf & Stock, 2014.

———. "Four Gifts of the American Church to the Universal Church." *New Theology Review* (Nov. 2003) 64–74.

———. *Jesus: Symbol of God.* Markyknoll, NY: Orbis, 1999.

———. "Lessons from an Extraordinary Era: Catholic Theology since Vatican II." *America Magazine* (March 2008) 11–16.

Herman, Judith L. *Trauma and Recovery: The Aftermath of Violence—From Domestic Abuse to Political Terror.* London: Hachette UK, 2015.

Hermans, C. A. M. "Abductive Hermeneutics." In *Hermeneutics and Religious Education*, edited by H. Lombaerts and D. Pollefeyt, 95–120. Bibliotheca Ephemeridum theologicarum Lovaniensium 180. Leuven: Peeters, 2004.

Holt, Stephanie, Helen Buckley, and Sadhbh Whelan. "The Impact of Exposure to Domestic Violence on Children and Young People: A Review of the Literature." *Child Abuse & Neglect* 32/8 (2008) 797–810.

Horton Anne L., and Judith A. Williamson, eds. *Abuse and Religion: When Praying Isn't Enough.* Lexington, MA: Heath, 1988.

Horton, A. L., M. M. Wilkins, and W. Wright. "Women Who Ended Abuse: What Religious Leaders and Religion Did for These Victims." In *Abuse and Religion: When Praying Isn't Enough*, edited by Anne L. Horton and Judith A. Williamson, 235–46. Lexington, MA: Heath, 1988.

House of Peace. "Finding Spiritual Strength." *Resurrection Story*, 2016.

———. "My Cross: HOPE." *Resurrection Story*, 2016.

———. "My Cross: My Strength." *Resurrection Story*, 2016.

———. "My Cross: The Grapevine, Love, and Life." *Resurrection Story*, 2016.

———. "My Cross: The Joy of Living." *Resurrection Story*, 2016.

———. "My Cross: The Love of God Reflected in Jesus and the Virgin Mary." *Resurrection Story*, 2016.

———. "My Cross: The Setting of the Sun." *Resurrection Story*, 2016.

———. "My Cross: Transformation." *Resurrection Story*, 2016.

Humphreys, Janice. "Spirituality and Distress in Sheltered Battered Women." *Journal of Nursing Scholarship* 32 (2000) 273–78.

International Theological Commission. "*Sensus Fidei* in the Life of the Church." The Vatican, 2014.

Isasi-Díaz, Ada María. *En la Lucha (In the Struggle): A Hispanic Women's Liberation Theology*. Minneapolis: Fortress, 1993.

———. *Mujerista Theology: A Theology for the Twenty-First Century*. Louisville: Westminster John Knox, 1996.

Jacobs, Janet L. "The Effects of Ritual Healing on Female Victims of Abuse: A Study of Empowerment and Transformation." *Sociological Analysis* 50 (1989) 265–79.

Jankowski, Peter J. "An Anabaptist-Mennonite Perspective of Intimate Partner Violence." In *Religion and Men's Violence against Women*, edited by Andy J. Johnson, 221–37. New York: Springer, 2015.

Jeanrond, Werner G. "From Resistance to Liberation Theology: German Theologians and the Non/Resistance to the National Socialist Regime." *Journal of Modern History* 64 (1992) 187–203.

Johnson, Elizabeth A. *Ask the Beasts: Darwin and the God of Love*. London: Black, 2014.

———. *Friends of God and Prophets: A Feminist Theological Reading of the Communion of Saints*. New York: Continuum, 1998.

———. *She Who Is: The Mystery of God in Feminist Theological Discourse*. New York: Crossroad, 1992.

Jones, Laura K., and Jenny L. Cureton. "Trauma Redefined in the DSM-5: Rationale and Implications for Counseling Practice." *Professional Counselor* 4 (2014) 257–71.

Jones, Serene. *Trauma and Grace: Theology in a Ruptured World*. Louisville: Westminster John Knox, 2009.

Jones, William R. "Theodicy: The Controlling Category for Black Theology." *Journal of Religious Thought* 30 (1973) 28–38.

Joynes, Christine E. "The Sound of Silence: Interpreting Mark 16:1–8 through the Centuries." *Interpretation* 65 (2011) 18–29.

Keshgegian, Flora A. *Redeeming Memories: A Theology of Healing and Transformation*. Nashville: Abingdon, 2000.

———. *Time for Hope: Practices for Living in Today's World*. New York: Continuum, 2006.

Kimmel, Michael S. "'Gender Symmetry' in Domestic Violence: A Substantive and Methodological Research Review." *Violence against Women* 8/11 (2002) 1332–63.

Knust, Jennifer Wright. *Unprotected Texts: The Bible's Surprising Contradictions about Sex and Desire.* New York: HarperCollins, 2011.

Kwok, Pui-lan. "Postcolonial Intervention in Political Theology." *Political Theology* 17 (2016) 223–25.

Levine, Peter A. *In an Unspoken Voice: How the Body Releases Trauma and Restores Goodness.* Berkeley: North Atlantic 2010.

Loue, Sana. "Family Violence and Abuse in the Context of Faith and Belief." In *Handbook of Religion and Spirituality in Social Work Practice and Research.* New York: Springer, 2017.

Marcus, Joel. *Mark 8–16.* Yale Anchor Bible. New Haven: Yale University Press, 2009.

Mariana. Interviewed by Ashley Theuring, House of Peace, Chicago, November 2016.

Martina. Interviewed by Ashley Theuring, House of Peace, Chicago, November 2016.

Max W., D. P. Rice, E. Finkelstein, R. A. Bardwell, and S. Leadbetter. "The Economic Toll of Intimate Partner Violence Against Women in the United States." *Violence Vict.* 19 (2004) 259–72.

Merton, Thomas. "The Woman Clothed with the Sun." In *New Seeds of Contemplation,* 170–78. Boston: Shambhala, 2003.

Metz, Johann Baptist. "Creative Hope." *CrossCurrents* 17/2 (1967) 171–79.

———. *Faith in History and Society: Toward a Practical Fundamental Theology.* Translated by David Smith. New York: Crossroad, 1980.

Mitchell, Joan L. *Beyond Fear and Silence: A Feminist-Literary Reading of Mark.* New York: Continuum, 2001.

Mitchem, Stephanie Y. "Womanists and (Unfinished) Constructions of Salvation." *Journal of Feminist Studies in Religion* 19 (2001) 85–100.

Mollica, Richard F. *Healing Invisible Wounds: Paths to Hope and Recovery in a Violent World.* Nashville: Vanderbilt University Press, 2008.

Moltmann, Jürgen. *A Broad Place: An Autobiography.* Translated by Margaret Kohl. Minneapolis: Fortress, 2008.

———. *Ethics of Hope.* Translated by Margaret Kohl. Minneapolis: Fortress, 2012.

———. *The Experiment Hope.* Edited and translated by Douglas Meeks. 1975. Reprint, Eugene, OR: Wipf & Stock, 2003.

———. *Theology of Hope: On the Ground and the Implications of a Christian Eschatology.* Translated by James W. Leitch. 1967. Reprint, Minneapolis: Fortress, 1993.

Moltmann, Jürgen, with Harvey Cox. *The Future of Hope: Theology as Eschatology.* New York: Herder & Herder, 1970.

Moscicke, Hans. "Priests, Stones, Temples, and Women: A Narratival and Feminist Analysis of Mark's Ending." *Conversations with the Biblical World* 33 (2013) n.p.

Murphy, Nancey, Julene Pommert, and Bonnie Vidrine. "Pentecostal and Charismatic Churches." In *Religion and Men's Violence Against Women,* edited by Andy J. Johnson, 283–99. New York: Springer, 2015.

Nash, Shondrah Tarrezz. "Changing of the Gods: Abused Christian Wives and their Hermeneutic Revision of Gender, Power, and Spousal Conduct." *Qualitative Sociology* 29 (2006) 195–209.

Nason-Clark, Nancy. *The Battered Wife: How Christians Confront Family Violence.* Louisville: Westminster John Knox, 1997.

———. "When Terror Strikes at Home: The Interface Between Religion and Domestic Violence." *Journal for the Scientific Study of Religion* 43 (2004) 303–10.

Nickelsburg, George W. E. *Resurrection, Immortality, and Eternal Life in Intertestamental Judaism and Early Christianity*. Expanded ed. Harvard Theological Studies. Cambridge: Harvard University Press, 2006.

Nogushi, Yuki. "Domestic Abuse Can Escalate in Pandemic and Continue Even If You Get Away." NPR, June 1, 2020. https://www.npr.org/sections/health-shots/2020/06/01/860739417/domestic-abuse-can-escalate-in-pandemic-and-continue-even-if-you-get-away/.

O'Collins, Gerald, SJ, and Daniel Kendall, SJ. "Mary Magdalene as Major Witness to Jesus' Resurrection." *Theological Studies* 48 (1987) 640–43.

Ormerod, Neil, "Sensus Fidei and Sociology: How Do We Find the Normative in the Empirical?" In *Learning from All the Faithful: A Contemporary Theology of the Sensus Fidei*, edited by Bradford E. Hinze and Peter C. Phan, 89–102. Eugene, OR: Pickwick Publications, 2016.

Osiek, Carolyn. "The Women at the Tomb: What Are They Doing There?." *Theological Studies* 53 (1997) 103–18.

Overcash, Wendy S., Lawrence G. Calhoun, Arnie Cann, and Richard G. Tedeschi. "Coping with Crises: An Examination of the Impact of Traumatic Events on Religious Beliefs." *The Journal of Genetic Psychology* 157 (1996) 455–64.

Ozaki, Reiko and Melanie D. Otis. "Gender Equality, Patriarchal Cultural Norms, and Perpetration of Intimate Partner Violence: Comparison of Male University Students in Asian and European Cultural Contexts." *Violence against Women*, 23/9 (2017) 1076–99.

Peirce, C. S. "How to Make Our Ideas Clear." In *The Nature of Truth*, edited by M. P. Lynch, 193–209. Cambridge: MIT Press, 2001.

Perilla, J. L. "Domestic Violence as a Human Rights Issue: The Case of Immigrant Latinos." *Hispanic Journal of Behavioral Sciences* 21 (1999) 107–33.

Pew Research Center. "Changing Faiths: Latinos and the Transformation of American Religion." Washington, DC: Pew Research Center, 2007.

Pineda-Madrid, Nancy. "Hope and Salvation in the Shadow of Tragedy." In *Hope: Promise, Possibility, and Fulfillment*. Edited by Richard Lennan and Nancy Pineda-Madrid. New York: Paulist, 2013.

———. "The Blessing of a Latino/a Religious Worldview." *Church* 23/4 (2007) 5–8.

———. "Responding to Social Suffering—Practices of Resistance." In *Suffering and Salvation in Ciudad Juárez*. Minneapolis: Fortress, 2011.

———. *Suffering and Salvation in Ciudad Juárez*. Minneapolis: Fortress, 2011.

Portier, William L. *Tradition and Incarnation: Foundations of Christian Theology*. New York: Paulist, 1994.

Ruether, Rosemary Radford. "The Western Religions Tradition and Violence Against Women in the Home." In *Christianity, Patriarchy and Abuse: A Feminist Critique*. Edited by Joanne Carlson Brown and Carole R. Bohn. New York: Pilgrim, 1989.

Rahner, Karl. *Foundations of Christian Faith: An Introduction to the Idea of Christianity*. New York: Crossroad, 1978.

———. *Hearer of the Word*. Translated by Andrew Tallon. New York: Continuum, 1994.

Rambo, Shelly. *Spirit and Trauma: A Theology of Remaining*. Westminster John Knox, 2010.

Sawicki, Marianne. "Making Jesus." In *A Feminist Companion to Mark*, edited by Amy-Jill Levine with Marianne Blickenstaff, 136–70. Feminist Companion to the New Testament and Early Christian Writings 2. Sheffield: Sheffield Academic, 2001.

Schüssler Fiorenza, Elisabeth. *In Memory of Her: Feminist Theological Reconstruction of Christian Origins,* New York: Crossroad, 1983.

———. *Jesus: Miriam's Child, Sophia's Prophet.* New York: Continuum, 1994.

Senter, Karolyn Elizabeth, and Karen Caldwell. "Spirituality and the Maintenance of Change: A Phenomenological Study of Women Who Leave Abusive Relationships." *Contemporary Family Therapy* 24 (2002) 543–64.

Sobrino, Jon. *Christ the Liberator: A View from the Victims.* Translated by Paul Burns. Maryknoll, NY: Orbis 2015.

———. *Christology at the Crossroads: A Latin American Approach.* Translated by John Drury. 1978. Eugene, OR: Wipf & Stock, 2002.

———. *Jesus the Liberator: A Historical Theological Reading of Jesus of Nazareth.* Translated by Paul Burns and Frances McDonagh. Maryknoll, NY: Orbis, 1993.

———. *No Salvation Outside the Poor: Prophetic–Utopian Essays.* Maryknoll, NY: Orbis 2008.

———. *Principle of Mercy: Taking the Crucified People from the Cross.* Maryknoll, NY: Orbis, 1994.

Snyder, C. Richard. "Hypothesis: There Is Hope." In *Handbook of Hope: Theory, Measures, and Applications,* edited by C. Richard Snyder, 3–24. Cambridge, MA: Academic Press, 2000.

Starkey A. "The Roman Catholic Church and Violence against Women." In *Religion and Men's Violence against Women,* edited by Andy J. Johnson, 177–93. New York: Springer, 2015.

Stegman, Thomas D., SJ, "'That You May Abound in Hope': St. Paul and Hope." In *Hope: Promise, Possibility and Fulfillment.* Edited by Richard Lennan and Nancy Pineda-Madrid. New York: Paulist, 2013.

Stephens, Rachel L., and Donald F. Walker. "Addressing Intimate Partner Violence in White Evangelical and Fundamentalist Churches." In *Religion and Men's Violence against Women,* edited by Andy J. Johnson, 207–20. New York: Springer, 2015.

Sympson, Susie S. "Rediscovering Hope: Understanding and Working with Survivors of Trauma." In *Handbook of Hope: Theory, Measures, and Applications,* edited by C. Richard Snyder, 285–300. Cambridge, MA: Academic Press, 2000.

Taub, Amanda. "A New Covid-19 Crisis: Domestic Abuse Rises Worldwide." *New York Times,* April 6, 2020. https://www.nytimes.com/2020/04/06/world/coronavirus-domestic-violence.html/.

Terrel, JoAnne Marie. *Power in the Blood? The Cross in the African America Experience.* Maryknoll, NY: Orbis. 1998.

Thomas, Linda. "Womanist Theology, Epistemology, and a New Anthropological Paradigm." *Cross Currents* 48/4 (1998). http://www.crosscurrents.org/thomas.htm.

Torre, Miguel A. de la. *Embracing Hopelessness.* Minneapolis: Fortress, 2017.

Townes, Emilie M. *Breaking the Fine Rain of Death: African American Health Issues and a Womanist Ethic of Care.* 1998. Reprint, Eugene, OR: Wipf & Stock, 2006.

———. *Womanist Justice, Womanist Hope.* AAR Academy Series 79. Atlanta: Scholars, 1993.

United States Conference of Catholic Bishops, *When I Call for Help.* Washington, DC: United States Conference of Catholic Bishops. http://www.usccb.org/issues-and-action/marriage-and-family/marriage/domestic-violence/when-i-call-for-help.cfm/.

Van der Kolk, Bessel. *The Body Keeps Score.* New York: Viking, 2014.

Walker, Alice. *In Search of Our Mothers' Gardens: Womanist Prose*. Boston: Houghton Mifflin Harcourt, 1983.

Walker, Donald F., et al. "Addressing Intimate Partner Violence in Rural Church Communities." In *Religion and Men's Violence against Women*, edited by Andy J. Johnson, 251–62. New York: Springer, 2015

Walters, Mikel L., and Caroline Lippy. "Intimate Partner Violence in LGBT Communities." In *The Wiley Handbook on the Psychology of Violence*, edited by Carlos A. Cuevas and Callie Marie Rennison, 695–714. Hoboken, NJ: Wiley Blackwell, 2016.

Watlington, Christina G., and Christopher M. Murphy. "The Roles of Religion and Spirituality among African American Survivors of Domestic Violence." *Journal of Clinical Psychology* 62 (2006) 837–57.

Weingarten, Kaethe. "Reasonable Hope: Construct, Clinical Applications, and Supports." *Family Process* 49 (2010) 5–25.

West, Traci C. *Wounds of the Spirit: Black Women, Violence, and Resistance Ethics*. New York: New York University Press, 1999.

Williams, Delores S. "Black Women's Surrogacy Experience." In *Cross Examinations: Readings on the Meaning of the Cross Today*. Edited by Marit Trelstad. Minneapolis: Fortress, 2006.

———. *Sisters in the Wilderness: The Challenge of Womanist God-Talk*. Maryknoll, NY: Orbis 2013.

———. "Womanist Theology: Black Women's Voices." In *The Womanist Reader: The First Quarter Century of Womanist Thought*. Edited by Layli Phillips. New York: Routledge, 1986.

Wolfteich, Claire E., ed, *Invitation to Practical Theology: Catholic Voices and Visions*. New York: Paulist, 2014.

Young-Eisendrath, Polly, and Demaris Weh. "The Fallacy of Individualism and Reasonable Violence against Women." In *Christianity, Patriarchy, and Abuse: A Feminist Critique*. Edited by Joanne Carlson Brown and Carole R Bohn. New York: Pilgrim, 1989.

Index